174.4 EVA
Corporate consciousness
: the new performance cul
Evans. Yvonne.
1030807

— 1116 .18

D1092534

Copyright © 2012 by Yvonne Evans.

All rights reserved. No part of this book may be used or reproduced by any means, graphic, electronic, or mechanical, including photocopying, recording, taping or by any information storage retrieval system without the written permission of the publisher except in the case of brief quotations embodied in critical articles and reviews.

Balboa Press books may be ordered through booksellers or by contacting:

Balboa Press
A Division of Hay House
1663 Liberty Drive
Bloomington, IN 47403
www.balboapress.com
1-(877) 407-4847

ISBN: 978-1-4525-4493-9 (sc)
ISBN: 978-1-4525-4494-6 (e)

Because of the dynamic nature of the Internet, any web addresses or links contained in this book may have changed since publication and may no longer be valid. The views expressed in this work are solely those of the author and do not necessarily reflect the views of the publisher, and the publisher hereby disclaims any responsibility for them.

The author of this book does not dispense medical advice or prescribe the use of any technique as a form of treatment for physical, emotional, or medical problems without the advice of a physician, either directly or indirectly. The intent of the author is only to offer information of a general nature to help you in your quest for emotional and spiritual well-being. In the event you use any of the information in this book for yourself, which is your constitutional right, the author and the publisher assume no responsibility for your actions.

Any people depicted in stock imagery provided by Thinkstock are models, and such images are being used for illustrative purposes only. Certain stock imagery © Thinkstock.

Printed in the United States of America

Balboa Press rev. date: 02/10/2012

CORPORATE
CONSCIOUSNESS

The New Performance Culture
"Consciousness is the New Currency"

By
YVONNE EVANS

"The new business culture sees us thriving, engaged, growing and inventive. This is the maturing of our times, from adolescence to adult-hood . . . , and not a moment too soon."

BALBOA.
PRESS

A DIVISION OF HAY HOUSE

INDEX

INTRODUCTION

I don't live in the corporate world, I "infiltrate" it regularly and work with it's less integrated behaviors. Just as the cities and communities about us have an underbelly, so too does the corporate entity. For the most part it manages to stay unaddressed, partially if not wholly disguised and in many cases actually supported and kept in place by the presiding authority.

To live in the corporate world means to have its value system, its measurements system and its lens of scrutiny, dictate and define your sense of self, your lens of experience and reality. I prefer measured boundaries of engagement and exposure. I prefer to potently interact with its consciousness in order to transform and evolve its complexity and then retreat. I prefer to hold fast to the steady, true core of my individuated value system and when called, to enter its corporate shadows, work the alchemy and quietly move away.

I see most of the people within this system day after day, struggle with these very issues. They strive to hold to their personal truths and values whilst having to function within an entity that opposes them.

You will realize by now that I am using a very different style of language. I ask you to be open and to engage with this style of dialogue in order to see the corporate world through a new lens.

The old paradigms and models have not succeeded. Debates of too much regulation, insufficient regulation, government control or market control, socialism or capitalism continue to rage. The answer cannot lie in any of these models or systems. They are rooted in a fundamental flaw. This flaw comes from the lack of understanding of how reality really operates. In other words, we are playing the wrong game on the wrong game board. It's like playing Monopoly on the Scrabble game board and neither are right.

We need to understand what the game board is and then understand how to play the game. A whole new paradigm of reality and therefore business and human potential is emerging. We need to re-evaluate how life works, how "we" work and then create the systems that maximize and leverage this knowledge into business and productivity.

When we do this, we will see a "falling away" of all of the symptoms of an inadequate and old paradigm. An inadequate and distorted paradigm that supported extremes of gain and loss; that cultivated systems of control, manipulation and ignorance. A model that ultimately engendered disease, stress, loss of productivity, loss of esteem, marginalization and alienation in the people conditioned to operate within it.

Cultures will emerge that are formed around a fuller understanding of what encourages and promotes genius, inspiration and aspiration in every human being. The losses that corporations, local and global communities suffer from disability leave and unfocused, distracted loss of engagement will become a thing of the past. This is not fantasy; it is an inevitability. We have broken through to a whole new realization of how life works. The books must be rewritten and a re-education will result. These are indeed exciting times.

This revolution will not happen overnight but it has already begun. We are seeing the collapse of the old models and the scramble to re-invent the new. The new sciences have been publishing material for some time that speaks to this paradigm change. A change in how we view ourselves, in how we view our world and in how reality functions. A re-education of humanity will take time. Our job is to empty our mental cups and open to a whole new way of operating. We are living in the time period of our own renaissance. We are challenged to take a quantum leap and in doing so, leave the comfort of the old platform behind. Just as our ancestors struggled with paradigm shifts from a flat earth to a round one, or a rotating earth and a central sun, we are in the midst of our own "orbit changer".

As is the norm during times of great intellectual shift, there is resistance and denial to be overcome. Yet with humanity's accelerated growth and learning in this age of information and with the urgent call for change and solution, I suspect we will move through the resistance phase quickly. We are tasked with generating innovative solutions to globally complex dynamics. The sooner we can avail ourselves of these discoveries, the sooner we can leverage the knowledge to foster innovation and solution.

Transforming our business world is essential. This *is* currently the "business" of all of us as we deal with the fall-out of the recent economic collapse. The shadow consciousness of certain executives and leaders has been illuminated and documented for all to see. The everyday person has been shaken awake, "eyes wide open" to a game play of dire consequence. There can be no doubt as to the need for a game changer. Waking up to the real playing board and learning how to play the only game there is, offers power and security.

Re-educating the culture of business and of human performance effectively requires us to look through a new lens. Transforming our business world into a system that is inherently healthy, productive, prosperous and sustainable requires that we indeed change our mental platforms and stand on an entirely different foundation.

A model has emerged that gives us the map for changing course and reaching that destination. This model emerges from the gritty and fundamental examination of CONSCIOUSNESS; consciousness as a model of the intelligence that we ARE. Consciousness as the power player in life that holds genius and creates outcome.

This strange new model gives us a powerful vehicle of discovery that will enable us to engage with genius, create with intention and have all peoples of the world living in bounty and prosperity. The polarized game of loss and gain is collapsed as a natural law takes over. There is plenty for all in this new game.

As we begin to learn about this game change, we will be challenged. We are re-introduced to concepts that seem to belong better in psychology, science or religious debate. Taking these concepts into a different context offers us a broader framework. The old paradigms came with very specific language and syntax. We are conditioned to accept the familiar structures. It is time to let this loosen and open to seeing, hearing and understanding things differently.

It is difficult to explain the paradigm without using concepts and words that will be uncomfortable and strange. Resistance will be a natural response. It is essential that you calm the resistance and keep going, as the learning arcs will eventually offer insight, clarity and power.

For so long we have operated with only one half of ourselves. Like using one hemisphere of our brain. Then we have developed and utilized a language-set to make this inadequate way of operating "function".

Yet our consciousness, that which we are, not only uses both hemispheres as a powerful dual—operating system but its lead driver is the hemisphere that we have shut down.

Therein lies the first and most important insight as to what has gone wrong. We have been operating or malfunctioning with half of our intelligence shut down. To shut down this particular intelligence has dire consequences because unfortunately for us, it is the intelligence that is the DRIVER, and that has the LEAD FUNCTIONING in our power base. It is this intelligence that holds our genius.

Imagine opening your computer everyday and turning it on as usual and going about your business, then suddenly discovering that there is a second power switch that you have neglected to turn on every day.

Imagine now, turning on that second power switch and watching your computer suddenly burst into life, color and dynamics, rebooting itself into a "super computer" with applications and configurations that are beyond your wildest dreams. How would you feel? Perhaps both excited and devastated? Devastated that you have wasted so much time and lost so much productivity and possibility operating on shutdown power. Excited because you can move beyond your boundaries of innovation and impact.

This is indeed how it is for us as humans. We have been operating with most of our power shut down. This power is an intelligence that holds understandings not known by the other consciousness. This power is an intelligence that holds our genius. We have been operating without our genius in play.

This genius intelligence we call feminine consciousness.

Now, before I lose you, I am not talking about females or gender in any way here. The word "feminine" is used here to denote the particular "nature" or function of something at a fundamental level.

Feminine consciousness resides in all males and females and simply refers to "energy" and "power" such as that in the ac/dc of electricity. It is like the magnetic, inward absorbing energy of the dc pole. The ac is a masculine pole and the dc is a feminine pole.

We have mostly been operating with the "masculine" consciousness within us, or the ac power or energy component.

This is a simplistic and reductive explanation to try and illustrate that the word "feminine" is denoting a type of function not a gender. Masculine consciousness is also not a gender description. It is a function that operates within both men and women. We all have masculine and feminine intelligence.I am deliberately choosing to keep using this word "feminine" as the descriptive because historically it speaks to so much.

Herein lies another key to understanding what has gone wrong. We have been conditioned historically to view everything that denotes femininity or femaleness, with distaste and to judge it as weak, ineffective and lacking power. Sadly, it is remarkable to witness how immaturely we as a collective still cringe, irk and whine over the word "feminine" or anything that might speak of something with matriarchal or motherly connotations.

This is not only immature and offensive but it is ignorant and stupid. It has served to disenfranchise us from this extraordinary power and genius. As was indeed the historical agenda, layered within a complex, convoluted explanation and story that is not for this book. Suffice to say here that the word feminine will be given its rightful place and we the collective just need to grow up and "get over it".

The natural state for us is to have combined access to BOTH our masculine and feminine intelligence with our Genius active and in the lead. A corrected driver and a well-developed masculine and feminine partnership is the hope for addressing our global challenges today. It is the way forward for our business and economic strategists and it is the lifeline for our collective being.

Feminine genius is indeed the driver and has the lead functioning in our psyche. It is expressed in the consciousness of "true" leaders but for the most, it has been relegated to the unconscious dungeons in the psyche. Shackled, muzzled, demeaned and ridiculed this aspect within each individual's unconscious now needs to be stirred.

If we are to address the elephant in the corporate culture and indeed in leadership in the political arena, then we must enter the dungeons of our unconscious and free its wisdom, discernment and power so that not only can we find that elusive balance so sought after in the business world but we can most importantly cause a global "changing of the guard." The genius within us must take the lead and be in the driver's seat into our new world. This is exactly the change I propose to catalyze in the corporate boardrooms and executive hallways; a changing of the guard.

CHAPTER ONE

WHAT IS CONSCIOUSNESS?

Consciousness exists within us as **awareness** and **perception**. It is the intelligence that operates all of our systems, our thinking and our feeling and it is US. We are consciousness. At varying expressions of simplicity and complexity this intelligence classically operates on three levels as the unconscious, sub conscious and conscious awareness. Fundamentally consciousness has a dual nature and in quantum physics and indeed in the Tao and in the eastern philosophies we hear of dualised consciousness as the Yin and Yang or masculine and feminine consciousness (not gender specific).

Quantum physicists see consciousness as residing in every cell of our body as intelligent particles of "light". They too see particles of consciousness as having ultimately two defining types of expression. One type of motion is light expressing outwardly and the second is light absorbing inwardly.

The Eastern traditions would call the light moving outward as masculine and the light absorbing inward as feminine. If

1

we were to substitute the word consciousness for information, we would say that as human beings, we are expressing information outwardly and absorbing information inwardly, like receiving and broadcasting systems.

In eastern religions we have the classic yin (feminine) and yang (masculine), model of consciousness and in the Sufi traditions, the Jewish religion and even in Christianity we have notions of feminine and masculine consciousness.

For this book, I prefer to concentrate on the explorations in quantum physics with its dualised light model and two types of informational energy, inward absorbing and outward expressing; stripping us back from the coarser chemical and biological models to a new science and energy model appeals to my need to move beyond religious or spiritual doctrines.

Also, as I explore the dualised nature of consciousness operating on three levels, unconscious, sub conscious and conscious and seek insight as to their evolving expression in human behavior, I will also call on Jungian psychotherapy and the collective unconscious with his concept of an evolving journey of becoming wise through the integration of our masculine and feminine nature which aligns with the new science and offers valuable context.

Though I believe Jung's notions of an anima and animus are close but not quite precisely accurate they assist us in recognizing that within both males and females lies masculine and feminine consciousness. I acknowledge the inherent parallels in some spiritual teachings and in the models of science as well as the analysis of Jung.

Consciousness, with its two fundamental "natures" of the feminine and masculine, resides within all males and females. We all have masculine and feminine intelligence.

Consciousness wants to evolve. It is the natural way of intelligence to take evolutionary steps of growth and development. Both the masculine and the feminine nature of consciousness wants to evolve from it's simple forms of expression to the more complex, it seeks to grow and develop.

MASCULINE CONSCIOUSNESS

If we map the evolution of behavior through the outward, masculine patterns, we see what we have come to call the **classic masculine archetypes**. Breaking these down to the simplest expressions we start with the following basic building blocks or components of masculine consciousness:—

It is behavior:—

- that *exerts outwardly*

- is an **outward expression** that is *visible* and *measurable*
- is *measurable outward* energy that is **mathematically quantifiable**
- it is **thinking in an ordered, linear, sequential way**

Let's think about these basics expressions of masculine intelligence as human character and behavior. Masculine consciousness is ordered. It is visible, tangible behavior such as outward actions and movement. It is the "doing-ness" of behavior because it is outward exerting. It is the simpler lens of "seeing is believing" and this lens of perception not only likes to be able to see to believe but it also values the measurable so it likes numbers and quantifiable existence.

DOING

Our masculine behavior of "doing" has evolved over time. In the beginning of humankind the doing was simple such as the hunting and gathering, the eating and sleeping and the pro-creation of survival.

As humans have evolved, we learned more complex forms of doing. Tools have evolved, skills and the basic thinking of "how to" has evolved. Think of the life of a child. Its external, outward doing begins with the simple tasks such as learning to crawl, then to walk, then to run. First they can grasp a finger, then trickier objects such as bottles, toys etc. Then they learn how to manipulate objects, how to play with them and use them. The child moves on to ever more complex "doing" such as riding a bike, skipping a rope, playing ball, using a computer. Further on, it becomes as complex as driving a car, operating a machine or flying an airplane; and so on and so on.

THINKING

Ordered, linear sequential thinking emerges as cognitive conscious mind develops. The infant learns over time to make links and equations in order to make things happen.

As this develops into further complexity the ordered thinking mind learns to count numbers, do math, analyze problems and complete tasks. In higher systems of thinking, the masculine mind is used to build community and society. Forms are created for co-habitation and survival.

Systems are necessary for civilizations to operate with order and control. From the many systems such as the supplying of water, the creation of road systems, the establishment of buildings, creating electricity and complex engineering systems, monetary systems and systems of government, the masculine intelligence is vital and valuable and has been used to "produce" since the beginning of time. (Another linear, measurable system.)

Both men and women have masculine consciousness and we see the classic archetypal behaviors of the provider, the protector or warrior. When we move to build anything in the world, when we move to provide for others, or ourselves to protect others, or ourselves we are using our masculine consciousness. Our warrior nature is our masculine expression.

As we evolve to more complexity we see more intricate and varied forms of building, providing and protecting. This occurs when the masculine nature evolves through a **continuing relationship of engagement** with the feminine nature. If it does not, the masculine nature remains as core, coarse expressions of thinking and doing.

FEMININE CONSCIOUSNESS

If we map the evolution of behavior through the inward, absorbing, feminine expression, we see what we have come to call the classic feminine archetypes. Breaking these down to simpler expressions we start with the basic core nature of feminine consciousness.

It is behavior and information:—

- that *absorbs inwardly*
- is an *inner intelligence* so it is *invisible* and therefore *immeasurable*
- is *immeasurable inward* energy that is *qualitative*
- it is *qualitative, inner world, abstract feeling* and *chaos*

Let's look at the core feminine expressions of human character and behavior. Inward absorption refers to inside perception of what is absorbed from around us. Inner intelligence refers to our "being-ness". The "quality" of our "being-ness" evolves from being an unconscious being at birth, to a sub conscious being in childhood to an ever more conscious and cognitive being as we grow.

FEELINGS

Our inner world also speaks to our feeling nature. As we evolve over time from the simpler primal expression of basic chemical feelings that urge procreation and those that cry out for food and water, to the more complex feelings such as affection, love, anger, sadness, fear, etc.

Feminine consciousness is of chaos. It IS the creator that absorbs and breaks down the old forms (in-formation) and births the new (in-formation). In our growth and development, we pass through several initiatory stages, from infancy to young childhood, to adolescence to adulthood.

In adulthood we pass through many archetypal transformations (if we are naturally evolving). For this to happen effectively we must die to the old self and allow from within a new self to be born; over and over again. This entire creative process is the feminine wisdom's domain. Feminine consciousness IS the creative and transformative energy.

IDENTITY

As I have said, our feminine intelligence as "being" has evolved over time. In the beginning the being of who we are was very unconscious. It was simply the instinctive and hormonal messages of being "male" or "female" that offered any sense of self-awareness.

As humans have evolved, our awareness of "being ness" has become more conscious and more complex. A child of today begins with no sense of either male or femaleness. The parental and societal cues and conditioning imposes this onto the consciousness of the child. As the child grows they develop awareness of deeper impulses of identity and begin to sort likes and dislikes and needs and wants with parental and societal expectations.

As they get older they may perhaps be exploring religious or spiritual identity, values, morals and ethics and ever-more complex explorations of their being-ness. So many variables are in play that impact how conscious and aware a person becomes in their personal growth.

Although in its' nature it functions as that which is chaos, the feminine intelligence is both birth and death. It is the chaos that breaks down the old order and brings in the new order. It is the chaos that kills off the old form to birth the new form. It is the chaos that takes an idea or a thought and breaks it apart for examination and consideration so that ideas, innovation and vision can emerge.

Successful, change requires feminine consciousness. To successfully create change whether it is within a culture, a system, or ourselves we must successfully partner our feminine consciousness and be willing to engage with chaos, death, uncertainty and transformation.

The classic archetypes of the nurturer, the creator and the perceiver are the core themes. When we move to nurture or care for anyone or anything in the world, when we move to create or birth new ideas or forms, when we can perceive an understanding, a dream or a solution for ourselves or others, we are using our feminine complexity.

The many obvious expressions of creativity are evident within such things as the beauty of architecture, the arts and its music, paintings, literature, poetry and dance, to name but a few examples. However this creative intelligence has a modus operandi that has critical applications across all spectrums.

The artist, the musician, the dancer, the philosopher and the writer are all seeking to access the higher levels of feminine intelligence to create masterpieces in expression. Access to this higher brilliance is via a zone of consciousness. Our ability to perceive, engage and be inwardly inspired comes from accessing this powerful ZONE. This zone is, to use corporate language, a zone of "high performance" where elite athletes reach for world records and where innovators reach for solution and invention.

It is here in this zone where our inner genius levels can be accessed. There are "pre-requisites" for accessing this zone and ultimately if we are doing the work of developing our masculine and feminine consciousness into balanced expression we have more access to this zone. As a collective humanity and as a global marketplace wanting renewal and re-invention the genius needs contact and avenues of expression.

HOW DO THE MASCULINE AND FEMININE WORK TOGETHER?

We think and feel together. They do not happen in isolation. What we commonly do however, is suppress the feeling. Thinking and feeling work best as a partnership where a person is aware of their thoughts and feelings at the same time and takes in the information of both systems.

Each system of consciousness offers information for sorting. By seeking understanding of both sets of information a person can cultivate deeper perception and insight about the presenting dynamic. Listening, being receptive and considered gives us access to inner tuition and to developing our inner intelligence by making it more conscious.

Analysis, ordered thinking through and questioning can then partner with the receptive intelligence to reach discovery, understanding or knowing.

Communication that takes place with both information systems offers more quantity and quality of insight; true understanding can take place. Consciousness as we have said needs to evolve and grow to ever more complex understanding. Working in partnership, there *is* evolution of understanding and awareness.

If the feelings and emotions that are present are suppressed in this process they stay in the body/being of the person. They await discovery and release into transformed understanding and new consciousness. Rather than a person moving towards their genius and climbing the ladder of higher awareness, they plateau and can entropy and slide backwards like a game of snakes and ladders.

CHAPTER TWO

VALUE SYSTEMS

The masculine consciousness needs the feminine wisdom's ability to "take in" information and understand it. It needs feminine consciousness to take in information and qualitatively evaluate it.

This means the ability to unpack the information with the "why's", the "what if's" of conscious consideration in order to judge its value and meaning. Masculine consciousness needs to learn to think through to ever-more complex levels of understanding and it needs the feminine powers of perception and sorting to come to a depth of understanding.

The consequences of our actions and choices and the understandings of complex relational dynamics within various given scenarios are birthed with this advanced perception.

This is an active act of engagement. As we can see with our own observations, there are many human beings who do not actively engage their thinking and absorbing of information in order to seek insight and understanding before acting. There are various reasons for this but for now we will look at the simple fact of a lack of will to actively reflect, digest and consider information before action.

PATRIARCHAL CULTURE

As a species, I believe we have plateaued many times in our evolution, failing to move beyond a certain level of consciousness. This is because we have valued the masculine consciousness in our nature so thoroughly and suppressed the feminine consciousness so successfully that we have failed to grow. The natural awareness and expression of our feelings, our intuition and our passions have been denied. The natural processing and transformation of our "feeling understandings" has been thwarted.

We have perpetuated a patriarchal culture of thinking and controlling with the ego; of strategizing, analyzing and rationalizing emotional and intuitive intelligence; of imbalanced values and systems. We have immersed ourselves in a culture of materialism at all costs where we act with little thought of wider consequence. In this value system the "ends justify the means" has ruled.

THE ENDS JUSTIFIES THE MEANS

When we worship all that is visible, tangible and quantifiable what happens to our value system is that we begin to cultivate an "ends justify the means" mentality. The bottom-line is all that matters. Witness the recent economic collapse with its reckless pursuit of profit at all cost. We cannot imagine a world where money has no currency. If our value system is polarized we can justify any and all actions as long as they achieve their ends.

What leads the way in a patriarchal (masculine) value system is not a consciousness of wise perception and mature authority but an imbalanced, myopic consciousness that does what it wants with insufficient regard for who or what it is "being" and who or what it is affecting.

Operating isolated from its feminine, this consciousness operates with large levels of denial and ignorance and uses the status symbols of its culture to denote success and superiority. Money, title, address, brand, association, and image are all that matters. If the economy collapses and all that is material are lost, such a person is exposed to a crisis of worth.

Who am I without my "things," my props?
Who am I without my money?
Who am I without my job, my title, and my work identity?

"Being the richest man in the cemetery doesn't matter to me.
Going to bed at night saying we've done something
wonderful, that's what matters to me."
Steve Jobs

Sadly, many people in the aftermath of a stock market crash take their own lives because of the pain and distress of such a confrontation. If we **only** value the accumulation of the material, the monetary and the tangible, we are at risk. Our identity and our self worth can become attached to these tangible materialisms. Our character can lack substance, integrity and coherence as the focus on the material takes over. Denial can become a close friend, developing a depth of being can be thwarted and more importantly, we fail to access our true power.

In truth, when consciousness is understood, this isolated value system is ignorant and promotes mediocrity. If however, these values are incorporated as part of an inclusive value system that is re-positioned to acknowledge genius as the ultimate driver and all that comes with the feminine value system as vital and necessary, a prosperous and abundant mind-set with a considered and wise lens can operate.

Feminine consciousness values "being". Self-knowledge, emotional intelligence, perception and innovation are of this value system. It values access to the "zone". The zone is the open door to passion and inspiration, it is the true power source that regenerates, invigorates and enlivens. It is the doorway to genius. Feminine consciousness values this passion and inspiration. It values relationships with self, with others and with the wider world.

Here, we see meaning and matters of the heart as valued and important. The feminine consciousness wants to be aligned with its true creative impulse and to be authentic in its expression. It seeks substance, truth and alliance.

CHAPTER THREE

THE MASCULINE AND THE FEMININE

Examining the two types of consciousness further, I have created the following two tables that describe the components or qualities and character traits of each type of creative intelligence.

There are many descriptions that can be added to each list but this will give you a broader understanding of them.

THE MASCULINE CONSCIOUSNESS
NOT GENDER SPECIFIC

Active	Structure	Product
Order	Reason	Outcomes
Doing	Intellect/logic	Profits
Thinking	Seeking	Competition
Control	Motivation	Comparison
Tangible	Generating	Attack
Measurable	System	Manifestation
Definable	Performance	Security
Linear	Duty	Image
Rational	Obligation	Status
Demanding	Providing	Shaping
Ideas	Father/	Forming
Tyranny	principle	Focus
Assert	Challenge	Passion
Extrovert	Struggle	Desire
Outer World	Willing	Instinct
Domination	Protecting	Meaning
Isolation	Defending	Understanding

The masculine expression is active and doing; it is the father principle in archetypal concepts. It is known as the mental or thinking consciousness and as it is developed it creates the established ego self.

The masculine is an outward exerting energy that pushes away as it expresses and in its extreme it seeks to isolate and dominate. It is the will of the mind and it is the shaping, focusing and forming energy of manifesting things in the world. It likes to control and create order. In it's extreme it can be a tyrant.

The masculine is dynamic outward motivation, it is exuberance that can be passionate and spirited.

Masculine consciousness is about linear, logical, sequential thinking. It operates mentally through the concrete and measures everything in numbers. At its least complex it is very "black and white". At this level the ego structure is still forming and the attention is firmly on self. The ability to recognize "others" and their reality is limited.

The simplest mind evolves from a "black and white" view of the world that makes simple polarized equations. This is the "either", "or" mentality that sees only the coarsest levels of reality.

As the mind develops it is challenged to move to ever-more complex forms of thinking through the feminine feeling world. It can move into perceiving variables and taking into account dynamics such as context, relationship and ramification and the more abstract thinking/feeling that leads to qualitative understanding.

When more fully developed in consciousness, the mind forms values and beliefs with its thinking and understanding. It moves from being egocentric to being aware of others if it is engaging the feminine mind. Awareness of others is a critical step in development that allows the mind to understand that it has impact on others and that there are consequences to actions and decisions. The mind has a range of possible understandings and awarenesses, dependant upon its level of emotional experience and process. If it does not engage the feminine, the egocentric personality remains.

Crude egocentric masculine consciousness with its need to control, isolate and dominate will create exclusivity and tyranny. It can bully and intimidate through rules and regulations, marginalization and disenfranchising. It's the "my way, or the highway" operator. The need to dominate and have control over others comes from having a limited ability to recognize and understand others. If a person has denied their emotional experience and failed to process their feelings to new understanding, their internal resources are sparse. Challenged to work out how to have an impact in the world, how to manipulate it and influence others who are in the world, such a consciousness reverts to control and domination.

If we were to look at this in the context of the corporate and political arenas it is a consciousness that leads through isolation and domination in its extremes, and it seeks to control.

It is the extreme masculine expression that values performance and competition and the "ends justifies the means". It is hierarchical and moves to compare and have power over. It is pre-occupied with itself and its power is defined as how much power it has over others and its world through domination. It can be attacking in its exerting and asserting energy.

Rules and regulations, systems and protocols keep order and control in place. Judging performance and results happens along a linear mental pathway of that which is measurable, definable and once again, controllable. Such a consciousness values profits, status and authority. Duty and an obligation to provide for others are masculine energies as are the need to create security in the world and a will to seek to protect and defend.

The more balanced masculine seeks to manifest things in the world and in the process, values competition, focused forecasting and goal setting. It will use higher intellect to generate systems and structures that help achieve desired outcomes. It can gather energy to do the necessary steps and stages in creation that implement the changes in shape and form.

It can brainstorm, run planning sessions and meetings that evaluate, decide and take action. It can generate systems for numbers in accounting practice and financial management. It can enter the multiple worlds of ideas and functioning with engineering and design or with the legal systems of rights, wrongs and consequences.

It can evolve into the complex world of the sciences and find solutions and new insights into our world and others. It can reach for higher understanding and awareness of reality and existence through the world of philosophy and theology. It can transcend its thinking process and experience alternate realities and perceptions.

Focused on the ego's formation, this consciousness can move to developing a personal identity with boundaries and structure. When the masculine expresses as desire and passion, it is that which is not necessarily sourced in love, but of a more primal and instinctive nature.

Sexual impulses and dynamics are shaped through a lens of image and possession. In a patriarchal culture we can see here the demonstrations of chauvinism in both men and women were people are sexually objectified and reduced.

The primal passions at simplistic levels can trigger a desire for conflict or war, or for mating and release without mattering or consideration. At complex levels, desire and passion can lead to finding ones talents and gifts. It can inform mattering and value for a person, shaping choices, values and personality.

THE FEMININE CONSCIOUSNESS
NOT GENDER SPECIFIC

Passive

Chaos

Receptive

Being

Feeling

Inclusive

Sensory

Love

Intuitive

Inner World

Nonlinear

Embracing

Reflection

Relationship

Aesthetics

Substance

Quality

Submit

Retreat

Empathy

Wisdom

Introversion

Co-operation

Mother/

principle

Birth

Death

Incubation

Dreaming

Nurturing

Family

Togetherness

Belonging

Accepting

Allowing

Stillness

Ease

Serendipity

Seasons/rhythms

Charity

Listening

Service

Artist

Intimacy

Play

Creativity

Receiving

Release

Transformation

Perceiving

Supporting

Mystery

Surrender

Flow

Fluidity

Abstraction

Aesthetics

Team

Imagination

Process

Spontaneity

Innovation

Feminine consciousness is "being". The feminine expression is passive and receptive. It is the mother principle in archetypal concepts. It is "feeling" consciousness and as it is developed it diminishes the role of the established ego-self that the masculine forms, as it births the authentic true self and the interconnectedness of "oneness". The true authentic self takes the seat of power away from the ego-self. The ego-self is a constructed persona that becomes the messenger of the inner power source.

The feminine is an inward, absorbing energy that pulls in and seeks to become one with. It is inclusive, accepting and relating. At its extreme and imbalanced expression it can seek to swallow and consume self or others. It is the emotions within and it is the feeling, imagining, creating energy of loving the world. It likes to allow the creative impulse within to emerge and have expression. It will allow the death of parts of Self to occur, to birth new aspects of Self and works with the chaos of the birth/death process.

The feminine's dynamism is "within" as it works with the alchemy of transformation. Like the seasons of the Earth, the inner world moves to seed, germinate, sprout and flourish new creative visions or forms. It can feel the flow and the cycles and rhythms of creating and manifesting. It also allows for the withering, decaying process of death and destruction and the re-generative process of life and creation.

The feminine dynamic is all feelings and emotions and ultimately it is Love. It is the inclusive, affectionate, embracing expression of human nature.

Feminine consciousness moves to support and nourish and is of the nature of inclusion. It creates qualitative experiences of belonging and mattering, of family, and team. It can surrender control to allow for the being-ness of others and create the space for them to thrive, grow, and be inspired and creative.

It will create relationship through understanding and knowing and feels acceptance and compassion for others.

In its move to relationship, feminine consciousness senses those around it and knows how to perceive beyond that which is immediately apparent. Communication "experts" say that 70% of communication is non-verbal. Feminine perception listens and sees beyond the obvious to subtle cues and sensing. When healthy in instinct and intuition it can gather information to understand what is being communicated at deeper levels.

This ability to perceive, to understand and know, creates a connection to others and can foster empathy. It is here that we can see feminine consciousness creating intimacy. Through deeper sensing, knowing and connection, relationships that are intimate and unifying can occur both within self and within relationship.

Although we have seen the "masculine" as being about formation of ego-self, feminine consciousness is responsible for the essential Self. Authentic being or the truer Self, is found through the stripping back of the ego and the transformation of its role in identity and control to that of messenger and "interface" from the inner Self' or "Soul" into the outer world reality. This occurs through the processing of emotions and the creation of a compassionate heart.

We tend to glance at this and think it's some religious or spiritual practice and fail to equate it with the every day functioning of "every day" person. Or we decide that because we are not spiritual or religious that this has no relevance to us. This is unfortunate because it is simply the natural evolutionary process of the maturation of human beings into genius.

For the purposes of this book, suffice to say that feminine consciousness is the Soul or truer Self that emerges from the journey through self-development to Self-realization. Your Soul has it's own agenda for you. Being aligned with your Soul's agenda equals "success". To be out of alignment with your Soul's agenda is to invite the ego life of stagnation, crisis and descent into mediocrity and loss.

If we were to look at the feminine in the context of the corporate and political arenas, it is a consciousness that leads through including others and creating alliance and team.

It will collaborate and gather information. Recognizing diversity it creates space to allow for cultural difference and cultural thriving. It is that which takes in the information and digests it to examine its relevance, meaning and consequences. Co-operation, collaboration and shared goals are the feminines values and it looks to pacify through peaceful means.

Feminine consciousness is not hierarchical as it does not seek to dominate, it seeks to include and create qualitative experience through relationship and co-operation. From this it creates the space for functioning. Creating a functional space where creativity can thrive according to culture and the uniqueness of the individual is it's objective.

It creates a culture of belonging and interconnectedness. As it is perceptive and discerning it uses more information in the decision and action taking process and can create an environment that allows for the needs of the culture.

Creativity, productivity and inspiration are not nourished through the too-rigid confines of regulation and control. A balance must be sought where systems are designed to foster and nourish creative energy. This is where feminine perception with its multiple levels of understanding can work with the specific needs of the culture, team or individual to create the space to thrive.

As the mother principle in archetypal concepts it is that which knows how to create thriving through attending to needs, allowing and receiving the uniqueness and expression of others. It nurtures, cares for and supports its people.

Further, feminine consciousness in leadership understands the cycles and rhythms of creative process. It works *with* the creative process through giving time for the various stages to occur; therefore co-operating with the productive process instead of controlling it.

Whilst the "masculine" is about "the ends justify the means" the feminine is about the "why" and the "how". The process itself and the journey that is undertaken, its morals and ethics, its consequences, are all important.

Concerned with the meaning and the why of actions and decisions it considers both the immediate and long-term consequences of propositions before it acts.

Consciousness when understood as being composed of two expressions or having a dualised nature, offers us many insights. Borrowing from the Jungian model of the anima (feminine) and animus (masculine) we can examine human nature when it is imbalanced and expressing more or less of one or the other.

Over Active Masculine Consciousness with Under Active Feminine Consciousness

We are all operating with one of our powers under-developed. Those that have developed more of their masculine consciousness and less of their feminine will display the following kinds of expressions.

Chauvinism

Bullishness

A male preference

Male valuing (within men *and* women)

Women—viewed as valuable for actions or form

(as sex objects, housewives, mothers, secretaries)

This imbalance creates a reality filled with form with no particular attention paid to content or context. An example of this is that its' not "how well did you do your job" but "what title do you have?" Its' not "what did you learn?", but "what grade did you get?" Its' not "how nice is the person you met?" but "what did they look like?" and "where do they live?" Its not, "does the work inspire you and ignite your passion,?" but how "much money does it offer you?"

This person can become like a de-humanized machine.

A person who feels but suppresses their feelings in order to control their functioning. There can be not only a negation of feelings but also a demeaning and denigration of them. Viewed as unacceptable, judged as signs of instability or weakness this person degrades their own feminine intelligence and that within others.

Relationships are based on superficial needs and having little substance or intimacy. Image is important with a low level of authentic expression and relating and higher levels of image and status play.

Controlling the body through a fear of losing the image, this person can push beyond critical signals from their body to rest, recover or attend to injury and as such, disrupt health, well-being and personal rhythms.

There is a denial of the inner world's messages and information and distraction is used to avoid engagement with feelings. (Off to work, off to a function etc etc)

Then there is the danger of being trapped and imprisoned by the image, status or mystique that one has generated. Having to maintain that image and superior status through controlling actions and behavior at all times to avoid exposure. This is alienating and isolating and will eventually lead to depression and crisis.

The masculine nature when extreme and does not have a developed feminine nature to balance it, behaves in a bullish and chauvinistic way. Its lens of reality is all about valuing form and action. Classically we see the patriarchal culture behave in a chauvinistic way with its denigration of the feminine nature in both men and women.

It will take action regardless of consequence as long as it caters to the bottom line. It values speed and rapid decision-making process and de-values the more deliberating and considered process.

Concerned with image and status, the chauvinistic nature is consumed with how it looks and with appearing superior or better than. It is not interested in the opinion of others unless that "other" is more "superior" than them or to be impressed or has something they want.

In an effort to avoid being exposed and in keeping the image of "better than" intact, the person makes decisions on activities based on this need. Rather than listening to the deeper impulses and guidance of the feminine wisdom it overrules this informant and seeks out places, people and activities that bolster image, create superficial feelings of importance and entertain and distract them from the inner world's deeper feelings. Here we see the ego-driven human being, driven by persona and surface level notions of how to live and be.

Over Active Feminine Consciousness
with Under Active Masculine Consciousness

Those that have developed more of their feminine consciousness and less of their masculine will display the following kinds of expressions.

Hatred for men, within men and women.
Hatred for masculine women. Women are the best.
Lots of content with no form.
(All this material but no where to put it.)
Eg: They have researched the book but do not get around to writing it. They are functioning in potentia, unable to transform their reality into results. There is the harboring of negative emotions that are not transmuted, keeping the blaming victim in place.

This imbalance creates the person whose emotions play out over and over again with no new insight and thus stalling their growth.

From this we see a stagnation of dreams and there can be self-delusion and distorted self-perception. Unfulfilled fantasies are prevalent with delusions of grandeur, delusions of success and those grand schemes that never manifest.

There can be a passive self-pity with martyr-hood and victim-hood. Too much being that creates a diminished Self. The denial of self can be so extreme that the person effectively stops living. This giving in to the destruction of the self is characterized in the movie "American Beauty" where the wife of the army husband vacantly stares throughout the majority of the movie and almost disappears in each scene.

When the feminine energy is either too much or too little without the essential ego formation of the masculine, it reacts the same way, as rage and destructiveness. Manipulations that are destructive and negative and a need to dominate and control can be demonstrated and there can be vengeance, jealousy and hatred expressed. There can be hurting for the sake of it.

The feminine nature when stunted and without a developed masculine nature to balance it, behaves in potentia. Its lens of reality is impacted by a weak foundation and structure. The ego base is under-developed and emotions are unable to be successfully felt, understood and transformed to new consciousness. As such a stagnation of growth can occur.

Emotions of the past can either be played out over and over again or are suppressed over and over again and may become toxic within the psyche. An aggressive, bitter or self-pitying victim-hood can be demonstrated with attempts to manipulate or intimidate to make things happen. Without the "backbone" of the masculine nature sufficiently developed, the ability to create things in the world is diminished.

A plateauing occurs with an inability to complete, follow through and ground creations. Spontaneous visions and dreams can emerge and yet the person remains "dreamy" and ungrounded due to this inability to take the steps to "make it all happen". It is a functioning in potentia, and creates stuck-ness and loss of productivity.

When the emotional consciousness within a being is impacted with a great deal of unresolved wounding and pain, a distorted lens of reality ensues.

Cattiness, criticizing, gossiping, belittling, being destructive and manipulative by negating the power of another, by using knowing, nurturing, seduction, sexuality, to create dependence, control, dominance are all toxic expressions of imbalanced feminine energy.

Using fear tactics, prophesizing nasty events, using the art of subtle persuasion to direct the flow or being the power behind the throne without being visible, without taking responsibility are also expressions of imbalance here.

In extremes, the classical anti-social, psychopathic expressions demonstrated. A toxicity of unresolved, untransformed emotions results in a skewed and destructive behavior.

In the business world we have all witnessed these patterns of behavior and expression in the people around us. We have observed leadership that is bullying and intimidating and we have observed people who exist "in-potentia" and seem to do very little but gossip or undermine the effective performance of their teams.

These are extreme examples of imbalance however with right examination we will see demonstrations of the under developed masculine and feminine in everyone. It is the human beings growth curve and we are always growing and re balancing our natures, if we are attending to right process.

Human behavior when expressing in a healthy and productive way needs to have a balance of the masculine and feminine consciousness in expression.

The Balanced Masculine and Feminine Consciousness

The balanced performer is dynamic. The dynamism is mostly internal and displayed externally through an intensity of being. The dynamically balanced person is not necessarily moving at a fast pace. The dynamism is in the spin of their consciousness. They are processing information from multiple sources and weighing and perceiving direction, decision and action against multiple scenarios. This person is centered, passionate and present.

They are conscious of each moment and they listen, interpret, relate and create consistently.

They are open to the visionary levels of their intelligence and ideas are expressed and grounded into reality The entrepreneurial nature is often there with an ability to follow through and create the environment and the right team to make a vision a reality.

They have a heightened sense of perception and knowing. There is a tremendous will and a power of putting that will into action. Self-awareness is evident with depth and substance, and there is awareness and an understanding of others.

Relationships are authentic, honest and there is a great capacity for intimacy and lovingness. There is the discovery of meaning to life and a deep understanding of that meaning. The imagination is highly developed and there is a depth of feeling, (all feelings) and there is strength of character that allows for the experience of great vulnerability.

They can conceive of solutions and of what needs to be done, and they can innovate, delegate and make the hard decisions based on sound consideration and knowledge.

Those in financial mind-sets will have researched and studied the relevant data, managed the figures and the shareholder interest and know the markets cyclical nature well enough to make wise calculation and strategy. They are grounded in a value system that is balanced and mature and see the wider picture of impact and causation. They see what is important and integral in the dynamics of situations and can cut through to the core of issues leading others to see beyond surface level issues into the deeper issues at stake.

There is a natural move to take on responsibility and to engage in the creative, productive and transformative issues at hand. Further, the conscience of that person has been developed and attended to as guardian and gatekeeper of decision and direction.

These people have a dignity and a personal "containment" of their authority and substance. They may lead with a quiet, considered style. They do not need the old bold demonstrations of "power". They do not need to strut or posture, they do not need to "keep up appearances". There is self-esteem and a self-respect that is inherently present.

However, few people have achieved such a balanced and well-developed consciousness as although it is a natural evolutionary process, it is not a pre-destined, automatic outcome. Everyone must work with his or her nature at becoming more conscious of their thinking and feeling, of being responsible and aligned with their truer nature.

We must be willing to feel the depths, examine the understandings and move towards more access to the zone of our genius.

Plateauing, entropy and atrophy is the more common choice of the collective. Doing what is necessary to get by and then relaxing into the evening to de-stress from it is the usual modus operandi. This is not a judgment simply the result of a world paradigm that has cultivated a culture that separates a person from their inner navigator. A culture that is fear-based and sees the world as "doing things to them" and outside of themselves. If we were all taught to listen to our inner intelligence and to seek out the clues of what ignites our enthusiasm and caring throughout the many stages of our life we would be in a coherent state of being, reaching, aspiring, feeling the reward of self fulfillment, of learning and growing.

Instead we have manipulated ourselves away from our true expression and existence; and so we compensate.

This imbalanced culture, is predominantly constructed with a patriarchal lens and value system. Feelings are demeaned and denied, so there is little room for the necessary transformation of feelings and emotions that facilitate the very shifting of that imbalance. The chauvinism of this culture encourages people to value the thinking and the doing and avoid deeper enquiry.

CHAPTER FOUR

The Patriarchal Culture

What does it look like when we diminish the feminine's value and see through a one-sided lens of consciousness? Although the two expressions of consciousness are within both genders there is the obvious demonstration of the devalued feminine as it is perceived in the female form. Generally speaking a female will have in expression more of the feminine consciousness though this is reductive. Many men also have well developed feminine intelligence and many women are equally as demeaning of the feminine energy as men and behave as "patriarchal daughters".

Throughout history we have been witness to inequality issues with regards to women. These issues still prevail today. A woman is still fighting for equal pay and for equal consideration in the work place. Although some will argue that women have made considerable progress in this matter, within the business world, the world of politics and a number of religious cultures, there is much evidence that this is not the case. Aside from the more obvious evidence there is the more subtle shadow of denigration of women that is visible within the corporate and political sectors not just characterized by financial inequality.

Women are still subjected to the chauvinism of sexual comments and innuendo and physically disparaged. A woman's voice is often systematically shut down to censor opposing opinion or to limit her authority. Bullying is very prevalent as the urge to intimidate and control goes untransformed.

A female who shows feelings or emotions or may be angered by discrimination or inappropriate behavior towards her may be labeled and judged as a "loose cannon". A common complaint of women is an insidious undermining and covert hostility towards them that can often be prevalent in the business culture.

Women can speak of being "set up", of being marginalized and disenfranchised, particularly if the woman is perceptive and forthright. She must learn to "play the game", "tow the line" and not cause waves or she is a "trouble maker". Her intuition can be ridiculed, and her emotional barometer and radar can be denigrated with disparaging comments.

Both women and men with well-developed feminine sensibilities can find it difficult to function well within a patriarchal culture. They are often the most innovative and productive people and they operate with a finely tuned consciousness.

In quantum physics we talk of people as being like receiving and broadcasting systems. The "receiving" being feminine, the "broadcasting" being masculine. The receiver functioning in the innovative psyche is often very sensitive. It requires a certain environment within which to function well and be productive. It can be very empathic and sponge-like. The receptor of such a person is like a large satellite dish. It feels and senses the energies and emotions of those around it and is impacted by this.

Being less boundaried due to becoming more integrated and more "at one with", the innovative person can be overwhelmed easily if not given space to tune into themselves and their creative genie (feminine consciousness). They need a specific environment in order to thrive. They may like colors in their space, music, flowers, scents, water features and art . . . or not. They may need natural light, good air and lots of stimulus. They may need a closed door.

Open plan offices are the new "in thing" within businesses but this is not always a wise move for many. There are those who need a confined and boundaried space in order to be productive.

The creative/innovative perceiver when faced with problems to solve may need to take the time to immerse in the dynamics of the problem, becoming "one with it" so to speak in order to find the real solution. They don't always work in a rational, linear, sequential way with their productive process. These people are capable of finding the "magic" in a next move.

They may not always work to a deadline and they shouldn't necessarily be bound to a "time card". Clocking into the office at 9 and out at 5 does not work well with these natures. They need freedom to move and flow with their own creative rhythms.

As an example, at 3.am they may suddenly understand what "needs to happen" and move into an inspired flurry of activity early in the morning.

They may need to go back to bed at 7 and get that lost few hours sleep. On waking, they may need to eat a particular food item, dress a particular way and listen to particular music or news on the way into work. Once there they may run meetings, set up what needs to be done and achieve three days work in one afternoon.

If they are "on a roll" they may stay at the workplace until quite late before moving into the next phase of their evening. Creative consciousness cannot be controlled and boxed. Creative consciousness needs freedom. It can be nourished and cultivated, it can be partnered to establish some consistency and momentum, but it cannot be controlled. Many internet start-ups have embraced this understanding and thrive accordingly.

The out-dated ego driven cultures don't know how to do this. They are not creative. They try to control the creative process but this simply shuts it down.

The word creative conjures notions such as knitting, drawing, or designing. However, I believe productivity that is real, aligned and fuelled from that alignment within is creativity. Changing our language from productive to creative opens the door to that aligned state asking us to seek out where our energy lies and what it's focus is. It shifts our awareness inside to the greater knowing. "Productive" as a word moves one to simply doing and takes the focus outside. Doing anything as long as it is productive could be . . . . sort the filing tray, tidy the desk, get a meeting scheduled, and be productive for productivities sake.

Creativity is an intelligent flow of energy within you. It "wants" to flow into your day. It wants to create, create, create. If you are plugged into it, it will guide you to your next focus. Tasks may get done in a different order but they will be done if they are important.

We shut down this flow for fear that we will just play golf all day or read a book. However when your relationship with your creative intelligence is established you are doing the right work within the right environment and with the right people. You are aligned. You are thriving and happy.

You are fulfilled. You are not avoiding and you are not controlling. You are engaged and passionate.

CONTROL

The patriarchal culture seeks control. Lacking an understanding of how to create a culture that fosters passionate, engaged people that develop and grow healthily, its controls through reward and punishment. Measurement occurs around rigid tangibility's of performance. With a limited lens of perception this culture then rewards imbalanced, shut down intelligence. The very act of control shuts off the genius within all of us.

The latest trend is to do performance reviews "daily".

This has come from the fear of market place collapse and the subsequent move to have more control. We have no easy solutions and we can't bear uncertainty and chaos so let's instigate more controls.

Control is an ego-driven process. It is of a reduced intelligence and serves to take productivity into assembly line mentality. This is not progress. This is short-term force for long-term loss. It is ignorant, myopic understanding that is far from true leadership.

The leader that understands the true nature of productivity as creativity puts its people into greater alignment with their true gifts and talents, their values and purpose and cultivates an environment of growth, and development, belonging and mattering. People want to come to their place of employment, they want to be productive because creativity is pouring from them as they are engaged, enthused and aligned.

This is much harder to create when you have not done the substantial work of maturing your knowledge to balanced perception. So there is the potential doom of recreating business cultures with the patriarchal value system and through the lens of control over and over again.

Devoid of much understanding of complex behavior, these leaders find it impossible to create a culture and an environment that allows for the thriving of diverse consciousness. Limited then to the ego-driven strategy of control through fear and intimidation, they "lead" by shutting down the natural avenues of creativity in the individual, reducing them to a game plan that serves to stress, disease and depress them.

In such a culture, there is little voicing of the need for change, of discontent or opposition as it is not welcomed and is often ridiculed and punished. Change is shut down.

Many cultures will pretend they welcome such a voice but this is often mere pantomime. Hidden behind a polished performance lies the same agenda and nature. Over time, those who work in such an environment lose respect for the leadership and if choosing to stay, learn how to play the game. They suppress their authentic selves and if they are not supported in their wider world will eventually lose touch with who they are.

A self-medicating pattern of alcohol, sex or—food can help with the pain, or a move into prescription or illegal drugs. Some drift into a depression that begins to swallow up their joy, their esteem and their spirit. Heart-attacks in men are on the increase, as are many of the cancers that attack a women's creative and reproductive body.

Often times when I consult in the corporate sector I can work with someone and connect him or her to a deeper, more authentic Self. I may not see those people again for a year as I move around the world with my practice. When I return to them I can be shocked at what I find. I find myself wondering "where have they gone?". They themselves, have not even registered that they are becoming lost to themselves again.

The corporate culture is filled with messages of how to look, behave and be. The patriarchal lens says that success looks a particular way, acts a particular way and does particular things. When you "live" in that world you begin conforming to those notions by manipulating yourself. You begin to dress accordingly, act accordingly and change accordingly. In a short period of time you lose yourself.

Rarely are you aware that you are lost. You don't know you're not there, because you are not listening to your feelings. Your feelings are whispering to you all the time about your discontent, your loss of energy, your restlessness, your distress; but you're not listening. Feelings are not to be acknowledged. Feelings have no value, certainly not at work, maybe in your private life but certainly not at work.

There is new wave of information that speaks of "bringing your whole self to work". I have consulted to such organizations that promote this. Yet, of course, in order to bring your whole self to work, there has to be a more open culture that allows for the uniqueness of who you are. If you bring your whole self to work, assuming that you are all there and intact, you are going to want to change a few things so that you can thrive and be more productive.

You may want to work with a different team of people who are more on your wavelength and you may want to move into a different office space. You may need to voice certain concerns you have, so that you can trust your leadership and thus feel able to relax into being who you are.

You may need to negotiate a different timetable or change your line of reporting so that you are being acknowledged or understood.

To bring your whole self to work, you need to feel good about yourself and where you work. You need to be able to voice and you need to feel that you are cared about.

Performance will then be maximized and the losses in sick leave, stress leave and everyday distraction will be lessened. For those who fear this model will create a "lazy, fun loving culture of anarchy" remember, that this is not about no accountability. If a person is not achieving their goals and being effective in their tasks they are held accountable. It is not about a "free ride" it is about understanding what promotes achievement and wellbeing and what doesn't.

I have consulted to one senior executive who described his office as a "sniper zone". The hostility and the discontent on that floor were palpable every time I got off the elevator. No one on that floor brought his or her whole selves to work. They operated from the shadow self and as with most organizations it is the corporate shadow that is far more present than the whole person.

The corporate shadow is what is really running the corporations and it is responsible for the disease and depression within the business world and for the failure of culture change programs. The corporate shadow has no interest in becoming whole.

On the contrary, it works very hard to stay unopposed and to manage the status quo. The shadow within any organization is that which is in evidence when you have an imbalance in the masculine and feminine consciousness. It will be on display through chauvinism and through the untransformed feelings of the feminine.

CHAPTER FIVE

The Corporate Shadow

When I consult to organizations, many have a mission statement on display that states what they are all about. Branding and spin are everywhere and for the most part this is the first thing I dismiss. There was one occasion where I accepted that what a group's mission statement was and what they were actually doing, were accurate. I was asked to consult to the department of defense in Australia in their more secret radar division.

Full of scientists, all quite high brow and intellectually dense, I had to chuckle when they announced that their mission statement was to "detect, deceive and destroy". What a refreshing change (at one level) and I mused at the time that this was close to being the truth for a number of other organizations I'd worked with.

The truth of most organizations and business entities is that the collective consciousness of the group has a percentage of conscious engagement, a percentage of sub conscious engagement and a whole lot of underground, unconscious levels of engagement. As the rule goes, that which you have not become aware of, owned, understood and evolved remains subconscious or unconscious in your behavior.

Within any corporate entity we find there are pockets of gossipy, undermining, backstabbing behavior. From the least harmless but unproductive, to the most harmful and damaging ones, gossiping and undermining are commonplace. At first glance we can see that this is everywhere and "so what?"

However, when a team of people are allowed to feed such a behavior it not only becomes a habitual waste of productivity and energy but it can progress to becoming hurtful and offensive to others. If left untransformed the productivity of a company devolves and entropies caused a drop in their ability to be profitable.

Gender hostilities are also evident in most corporate entities. Here, often hidden in the shadows, insults and sexual slurs are expressed amongst agreeing groups; sexual preferences are denigrated and become the justification for harsh judgments or ridicule.

One organization I consulted to had a senior executive who has a team of people who worked 'for" him. Several of the women were gay. In the company of the women on his team he charmed, courted and cooed with them. Behind other doors he sniggered and offensively spoke of them disparagingly. Others "joined" in to align themselves with their "boss" and before long the hostile tone seeped into the team dynamics. Internet emails and then jokes and gags were dispatched for all to laugh at. The web of denigration spread to off–site meetings.

After complaints to senior management were dismissed and two women were told to "toughen up" the bullying worsened. The more they all got away with this the "darker" the tone became.

Eventually one of the women after leaving the office upset from an incident, crashed her car in a serious accident rendering her a paraplegic. No one from senior management visited her at the hospital. The other woman chose to walk away from the corporate sector completely after years of study and investment in her career.

A male executive in the same firm who was suspected of being gay was also repeatedly stone walled by the male executives on his floor as they openly demonstrated their contempt. This man was not gay, he was a dignified, productive and very engaged career person who didn't join in the "bully boy" tactics of his peers. To manage his day and his work he had to isolate himself and close a bubble of containment around his focus.

The senior executive tone fed and supported those who spent their days destructively attacking the most productive, focused and career-minded people on staff and effectively marginalized and shut them down.

I once sat with a senior female executive who had been the close confidante and good friend of the male CEO of the organization where she worked. A long time high achieving member of this firm, she was also the "right-hand power" of another high profile senior at the firm who was headhunted to another company.

When passed over this for high profile job and forced to accept a male "boss" who had the lesser qualifications and fewer years of experience, she licked her wounds and vowed to move on and do a great job for her new boss. Over an 18 month period, her new boss forgot to tell her about important meetings, sent memos to everyone but her, began to put his name to much of her work and systematically began eroding her confidence in her own abilities. It happened so subtly that she didn't know why she was feeling so distressed and so incompetent and out of sorts until she witnessed her performance review. Accusations and judgments that were unjust, and blatantly untrue sent her seeking answers.

She took her case to her good friend the CEO of the firm. Not only was he a good friend but also her husband was on his executive team. Explaining her distress and her twelve months of treatment to him he responded coldly with little support. Citing his workload and an unwillingness to give any of his focus to the matter, he further suggested that perhaps her work was no longer up to the mark. Stunned at this turn-around from the CEO and his changed demeanor, she left his office. How could she suddenly go from 16 years of being a highly regarded employee to an unappreciated "incompetent" in just 12 months?

Overnight she came to a clear-eyed understanding of the unfair treatment she was receiving. She insisted on seeing her "good friend" the CEO again.

Explaining her understanding of what had and was taking place she notified him that she would not be seeking legal avenues if she were taken care of appropriately.

Condescendingly he placed his arm around her shoulder and suggested that she didn't need much restitution because her husband was on a good salary and that he would take care of her. Stunned for a second time she said to him, "I thought that you and I were good friends?" To which he replied, "you were always more fond of me than I was of you".

Known for being such a gentle soul, for her generous nature, her wonderful listening skills and her hard work, this kind-hearted woman was devastated. Wanting to not make trouble, she took a reduced package and left.

She had been so loyal to the firm where she had also met her partner and truly believed that she had a dear friendship with the CEO. Didn't they all go out to social events together? Didn't he always call on her when he needed an ear? A few months later, on her partner's arm at a dinner at the CEO's home, he ignored her presence.

Whether hidden to most and visible to few, or the other way around, the corporate cultural shadow needs to be attended to and the leadership within an organization needs to be the first to do the work of transforming shadowy consciousness into clean expressions of more integrated behavior.

At a basic level, we need to move beyond what I see as an emotional adolescence so that interactions with others can be respectful and transparent. At a fundamental level, we need to seed a culture where we self examine our behavior, our motives and our agendas and take responsibility for who we are and how we impact.

Naturally, there are those who are least conscious who find such a task daunting and will not move to develop their nature. This is where leadership becomes essential. The leader should be the most conscious of a group and therefore able to inspire and guide others to do the work of self-examination. Too often however, leaders are not the most conscious member of a group but merely the ones who are better at playing the game.

A common issue that is visible with many business leaders is a shame/blame dynamic. Those leaders who were parented with a measure of shaming and humiliation as a punitive and motivating tactic carry within them a fear of making mistakes and a fear of being "found out".

With this leader the game becomes about shaming, blaming and humiliating others. When mistakes are made or when performance needs improving, managers holding a shame pattern, will move to blame others and to motivate their teams through shame-based intimidation and humiliation. They repeat the way that they were parented often for their entire career. When challenged they will defend their "style" as "tough" and necessary and fail to see that there is anything wrong with such a method.

The only way to transform this kind of leader is to first address the shame that they are holding within themselves through having them find discovery about their upbringing. Through examining and integrating the learning's and insights from this discovery process, the shame is replaced with self acceptance and compassion. The leader can then approach the task of leading and guiding others from a more respectful position with a more complex understanding of how to be responsible and empower others.

The feminine consciousness asks that a leader do the work of transforming their less integrated behaviors to greater wholeness and to encourage a culture where people can evolve and grow as human beings, sustaining the productive and creative energies in the corporate entity.

CHAPTER SIX

Consciousness as Power

To understand how to transform ourselves and our businesses into a balanced reflection of integrated consciousness, we need to touch lightly on quantum physics and then expand into how power itself evolves within us.

First, we need to move beyond the concept of seeing ourselves as biological and chemical entities, to exploring ourselves as **a system of energy**.

I will expand on it broadly as **"the awareness that resides in the body that can hold various beliefs, values, perceptions conditionings and understandings."** This awareness is not static and at its very core it is designed to evolve to ever-more complex information systems.

Beliefs, values, perceptions, conditionings and understandings are meant to change and evolve over time.

Freeman Dyson won the Fermi Prize in physics for his theory that consciousness is a "cloud of charged particles of light." Here we find a concept that is tricky to grasp at first glance. Quantum sciences take us beyond the physical reality into **the "energetic reality" of who we are.**

Quantum sciences with its new measuring and observing devices reveals to us that we are not solid and that indeed nothing is solid in this world. Everything is composed of vibrating particles.

Further, these vibrating particles have
an electrical and a magnetic nature.
Fields of electro-magnetic particles come together
to create form and outcome.

Now before I lose you with all of your resistances urging you to put the book down, let me say that I do not intend in this book to enter into a scientific discourse to prove quantum physics. I will stick to the "simple," basic insights that help you take a step into understanding how consciousness is the big player.

The next thing to understand about consciousness is that it is a vibratory field of electro-magnetic energy. We as human beings are composed of a vibrating field of electro-magnetic energy that both attracts and repels other vibrating fields of energy.

Forms can have very low "frequencies" of electro-magnetic vibration or range up to very high "frequencies" of electromagnetic vibration. Human beings are highly electro-magnetic. Illness, dis–ease and stress can deplete our "energy" thus lessening for a time our "attractive" capability.

Our consciousness, our mental and emotional and spiritual intelligence is "of this field". Or more correctly, our "field of attractive energy" is "of our consciousness". Let me leap to a simplified summary . . . .

> The intelligence that we are composed of
> is a field of vibrating energy
> that creates our reality.
> It electro-magnetically attracts and repels
> our reality and our results in life.

MASTER YOUR FIELD
MASTER YOUR LIFE

Understanding and becoming "conscious" of how we produce and create our results and our successes and failures with our consciousness is the new game to master.

> We are "at cause" in our life.
> Our resonant consciousness is "at cause".

In the world around us, as the familiar foundations of old supports crumble and fall away, the only security we have is with mastering the productivity of our consciousness. If our consciousness produces our results and our reality, mastering it makes sense.

I use the word "mastering" loosely however. Our business value system loves words like "master" and "control". In truth however, the intelligence that is our consciousness is not controllable. Mastering such an intelligence is really about consciously working in partnership with it. Our greatest tool for impacting our creative field of intelligence is the tool of active transformation.

In our business arena it is not the norm to engage in acts of transformation. In our business cultures we generally operate in a reactive or manipulative and strategic fashion to work the chessboard of profit and loss.

Where we do see a focused valuing of active transformation is in the arena of elite sports. Coaches and world-class sports people consistently work to find ways to transform and improve performance. Depending upon the nature of the sport, there can be sports psychologists, physical therapy professionals, diet and nutritional experts and motivational leaders, all engaged in shifting performance to elite levels of success. The zone of high performance is a highly conscious, self-steering state where intended success is realized. We must become partnered co-creators with this zone and take responsibility for creating the successes and the reality we desire.

We are in the midst of a revolution of a similar magnitude to that of the paradigm shift from a flat earth to a spherical one. Human beings have believed for so long that the way to make things happen in this spherical world is to move things around mechanically and physically. Rational, linear logical causation has been the modus operandi.

We need to move to a more complex realization that reality is created more dynamically through mastering the attractive field that we are. It is my belief that the challenges that we face today cannot be resolved through the application of the same mechanics. We must evolve to a more mature and wise awareness of what is our nature and start operating as masters of our reality. Not in an isolated and ego-based positioning but in a coherent, inclusive and relational engagement with truth.

Coherent, high levels of consciousness within a human being operate at their core with an inherent knowing of their relationship to all that is in existence. For the multiple fields of vibrating electro-magnetic energy that exist within all forms and are not separate from each other. There is One unified field that encompasses us all. If you ponder this for a moment, there is great leverage in that realization. There is power in one individual to affect the whole field of humanity.

We are in revolutionary times . . . . our world has changed and so too has our business landscape. In this climate of heightened instability, the chaos and turbulence of these times insists that we learn quickly what the new rules are to secure success.

The new world paradigm shows an interconnected web of relationships all existing in an electro-magnetic vibratory field of consciousness. Our perceptions, our beliefs our emotions and our understandings are reflected in this all encompassing field, showing up in our world reality.

> "There is no place in this new kind of physics
> both for the Field and Matter,
> for the Field is the only Reality."
> Albert Einstein

Einstein first coined the unified field theory and he and many other scientists have attempted to create a formula for a single field of existence.

Regardless, so many people worldwide have experienced this single field or unified field of creation and yogis and adepts who master the mind and "at oneness" have known and experienced this field as a reality.

Understanding this new reality paradigm begins with learning this new language and then learning to view ourselves and our world through a new lens.

Mastering this new way of conscious operation will take humankind a long time. Staying in the cynical and resistant mind-set and refusing to learn this new way of understanding our world and ourselves is a choice that some will inevitably make.

We must move to a new complexity in order to move forward with greater certainty and security. It can be too easy to condemn this new paradigm and fail to examine the powerful truth of what is being presented.

However, opening to the new language and being willing to question, explore and evolve our mindset can offer us the security of being on the leading edge of business and life creation.

AN OLD TRUTH

The new physics and the research scientists within such organizations as the military and the intelligence communities of various governments have for a long time run tests that verify this new paradigm of reality creation.

As early as the 1800s double split testing has shown scientists that the act of observing reality particles, changes the behavior of them according to the observers expectations or intentions.

Many modern day scientific studies have occurred since that time including an Israeli test at the Weizmann Institute of Science. Again, these tests showed that reality particles are affected by the act of being observed.[1]

Further, the tests illustrated that the longer the particles were watched or observed, the greater the affect. Such a realization has powerful implications. However most of the scientific community has for more than two hundred years kept this in the ponderable realm of intellect, academia and scientific debate.

What we need is for this insight to become practicable and applicable in the everyday world. Schools and all levels within the education system need to be introduced to the new sciences so that intentional reality can be explored and practiced. All creative and productive groups need to avail themselves of this realization and become conscious explorers in a truer and more dynamic approach to get results.

For so long now we have sleepily accepted a notion of a world where we are all isolated biological entities and where "things are done to us" and where we can become victim to "outside forces" that can impact us.

---

1 Nature magazine February 26, 1998 (Vol. 391, pp. 871–874)

Fearfully generated, we have been conditioned to accept this untruth and so we live believing we are powerless to so much and therefore we cannot trust life or ourselves. This becomes a self-perpetuating, self-fulfilling prophecy as the more we expect or even unconsciously believe life to be fearful the more fearful a reality we create; see the trap?

We need to learn about transforming our fears and conditioned limited expectations within our sub conscious and unconscious fields so that they are NOT creating our reality and once transformed, move to consciously and successfully creating with abundant intent and expectation.

To minimize the tragedies and the losses of our recent collapse, we must quickly avail ourselves of these new insights. We need to understand this new success paradigm and learn how to become deliberate, conscious creators.

Theory will no longer suffice as the stakes are high. We must begin to take individual responsibility for authoring our life. We must teach our children how to use their field of consciousness so that they can more elegantly move forward into this new world paradigm.

Business is no different. You may be reading this and thinking, "what does this have to do with business?" It has everything to do with business. In fact, perhaps it is more essential for business to grasp this realization than any other arena. In today's economic chaos so many people have found themselves homeless and "destitute". We all know that being able to "make money" offers security and reward in our system of exchange.

Businesses are being challenged in the changing global market place to sustain their relevance and profitability. The work arena itself needs to change its paradigm of operation rapidly so that it can move from being the victim of outside forces to the creator of a new platform.

So many are being called to "start all over again" and the fastest way to do this is to "get real" and "wake up" to the ultimate realization; what you focus on and expect, you get.

Conscious productivity is now the star player in this game of success, in business and in life.

Highly conscious organizations that invest in the continued learning and growth of its people will have long-term productivity, profitability and sustainability.

It is imperative now, that we move from proving something intellectually to understanding it practically and demonstrating it in our way of being and doing. Chaos (possibility) will be at the mercy of colliding unconscious forces until conscious steering chooses a new order (form).

(Now I am simplifying here. The "uncertainty principle" and chaos theory invite a whole other complexity into the conversation here but we will suffice with keeping it simple.)

Moves to regulate banks and financial practices in corporations are a move to address the problems at a systemic level. "People" are what run organizations and their collective fears, limitations and beliefs will produce results.

What we really need is to have a transformation in the mind-set of leaders and business cultures. We must build new cultures in business that invest in the consciousness of its people and encourage the thriving accessibility of the zone of highly productive experience. We must transform the internal raw materials of our people capital and promote a culture of personal development.

Productivity needs to be understood at a deeper level and the creation of the necessary environment that fosters true productivity and success must occur. This is where the business culture comes into being an essential component of success.

Leaders in business must rapidly mature their intellectual complexity and their emotional ecology to be of the resonant (vibratory) consciousness that allows for the intention and expectation of results. Leaders must also have the necessary understanding and the ability to continually transform the emotional mind-sets of their teams. Each resonant level of consciousness has threshold that limits its success. To achieve higher levels of success (whatever your value system defines as success) you must hold higher consciousness and its corresponding attractive resonance. Busting the thresholds and plateaus of success along with clear and focused intent create deliberate results.

The mechanics of success
is now understood in a new light
requiring a re-education of our mindsets.

We must learn how to access the zone within ourselves and to then transfer that ability to our families, our teams and our executive, whilst creating the space and the environment to sustain it.

For some in business and leadership these understandings will seem familiar and innate as these people may already have a consciousness that is composed of successful beliefs and being in the zone has also been achieved unconsciously.

They have a resonant field that contains optimal beliefs and conditioning and a high threshold for attracting success. Their internal self-image is strong and of good self-esteem and self-valuing. Place such a person in a career that is their passion and you have the natural state for Zone access.

Those who have effectively undertaken personal development and transformation will also understand the components of highly productive realities. That is, if they too have discovered what they care about and what kind of work brings them joy and "lights them up".

Yet there are substantial learning's that can still be offered to those that already work in the Zone that can move them to an even more powerful expression of success, making them true leaders in this movement of change. Business cultures are in dire need of new leadership to create the right landscape to lift productivity and sustain it healthily.

Hostile cultures that motivate through fear and mistrust will find they create business results that are far from high yield.

Struggle and discord within the culture will sap energy and redirect it into producing more of what it fears and expects: struggle.

Business cultures must become agile and effective in transforming fear. Fear in so many ways is now the ultimate enemy. Previously fear was used by those leaders of lesser consciousness as an easy form of manipulation.

When there is insufficient understanding of human behavior, control through fear becomes the only resource, the only expression of "power".

To have highly productive cultures "fear" is reckoned with and transformed into enthusiasm and the enabling of skilled, resourceful competency. Manipulation and control are lower consciousness expressions and serve to pull a culture into a subsequently low productivity levels. It is perhaps impossible for there not to be some forms of manipulation and control in business but the culture needs to be driven for the most part through meaningful engagement, with a transformational model that allows for access to the zone of high enthusiasm and aspiration.

When consciousness is not encouraged to evolve, control is more easily achieved. Power over others is more easily attained. The path to freedom and personal power is the path of evolving your consciousness. We are witnessing the global push for freedom in many countries and the call for the ability to create personal prosperity and abundance.

Consciousness is meant to evolve to ever-more complex levels of understanding. It is not meant to plateau and become stagnant and atrophy or become toxic. Consciousness wants to understand more and thus *become* more. Evolution means creating and producing at ever-more productive levels of expression and wholeness. It does not want to be controlled, it wants freedom and support to grow.

CHAPTER SEVEN

YOUR RESONANCE IS AT CAUSE

So lets recap and expand on consciousness. In a simple context it is the "awareness" that resides within us.

This awareness is composed of:

- intellectual and emotional potential
- intellectual and emotional understanding
- simple and complex levels of perception
- simple and complex levels of conception
- values, beliefs and impulses
- imagination, will, emergent insights,
- inspiration
- love
- it has electro-magnetic properties
- is of particle/waves/ and light
- pendulum/spin motion with frequencies and resonance

Consciousness as light and energy in motion behaves like a cone with a swinging emotional and mental pendulum. When the pendulum within that cone comes to centre and into present-state being, it can access an elite Zone. This zone is the state of high performance and genius.

Our beliefs, our model of the world and our self-image are imprinted in our subconscious and unconscious minds as mental and emotional experience and memories. As consciousness is of resonant vibration and frequency, mental and emotional imprints impact resonance. Our resonance is what attracts our reality.

The less polarized and the more unified or integrated our mental and emotional understanding the more unlimited our attractive abilities.

The more unlimited our beliefs and model of the world, the more loving and worthy our self-image, and the more joy and passion in our activities, the more genius we can access within this Zone.

The Cone of Consciousness

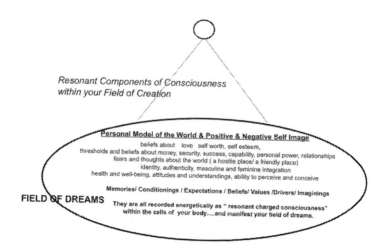

Resonant Components of Consciousness within your Field of Creation

Personal Model of the World & Positive & Negative Self Image
beliefs about   love   self worth, self esteem,
thresholds and beliefs about money, security, success, capability, personal power, relationships
fears and thoughts about the world (a hostile place/ a friendly place)
identity, authenticity, masculine and feminine integration
health and well-being, attitudes and understandings, ability to perceive and conceive

Memories/ Conditionings / Expectations / Beliefs/ Values /Drivers/ Imaginings

FIELD OF DREAMS

They are all recorded energetically as " resonant charged consciousness"
within the cells of your body....and manifest your field of dreams.

The model explained:

Our consciousness and its corresponding vibratory resonance is "at cause" in our life. Our resonant cone of consciousness is composed of all that you see itemized within the elliptical sphere above. Our conditioned values, beliefs, expectations and personal model of the world are magnetic attractors.

Further, our sense of self-image both positive and negative with our memories and experiences of emotional hurts and rewards and of our conditionings from childhood, are also magnetic attractors. This field of electro-magnetic beliefs and values, good and bad self-images, expectations and "patterning's" limit and attract our results and our experiences in our life.

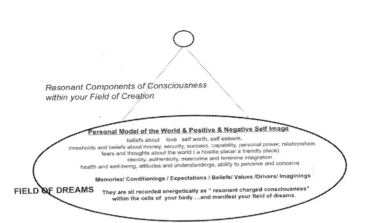

The Cone of Consciousness

Resonant Components of Consciousness
within your Field of Creation

Personal Model of the World & Positive & Negative Self Image
beliefs about   love self worth, self esteem,
thresholds and beliefs about money, security, success, capability, personal power, relationships
fears and thoughts about the world (a hostile place/ a friendly place)
identity, authenticity, masculine and feminine integration
health and well-being, attitudes and understandings, ability to perceive and conceive

Memories/ Conditionings / Expectations / Beliefs/ Values /Drivers/ Imaginings
FIELD OF DREAMS   They are all recorded energetically as " resonant charged consciousness"
within the cells of your body....and manifest your field of dreams.

How is it the power in business?

Collectively, our business culture is filled with multiple mindsets of consciousness all existing within a giant electro-magnetic field of creation that repels and attracts our business entities results. The resonant consciousness of our culture is "at cause" in our business.

Generally we assume that the chief executives of an organization or those that are the vision holders have a more complex and "higher" consciousness and resonance than those who report to them.

The Corporate
Collective Cone of
Consciousness

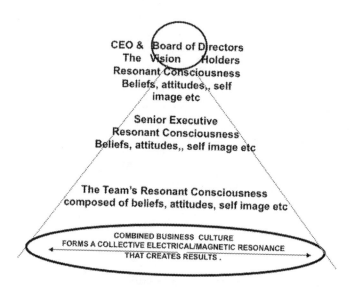

Here we see the CEO and the vision holders at the top of the cone illustrating a higher end of consciousness followed by the senior executives then teams of employees moving down to the lower and wider end of the cone.

Consciousness when existing at a higher level, has integrated and processed much of its emotional nature. There is therefore less swing in their emotions and judgments.

As the cone widens towards the base of the model, it is illustrating those people who have integrated less of their emotional nature and have a mindset that is very black and white and either/or. There is more "swing" in the pendulum of their emotions and therefore less focus and greater distraction.

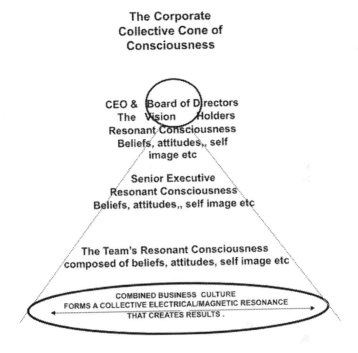

The Corporate Collective Cone of Consciousness

CEO & Board of Directors
The Vision Holders
Resonant Consciousness
Beliefs, attitudes,, self image etc

Senior Executive
Resonant Consciousness
Beliefs, attitudes,, self image etc

The Team's Resonant Consciousness
composed of beliefs, attitudes, self image etc

COMBINED BUSINESS CULTURE
FORMS A COLLECTIVE ELECTRICAL/MAGNETIC RESONANCE
THAT CREATES RESULTS .

To change our results in business we must change our resonant consciousness. Business groups attempt to do this when they instigate training and development programs or terminate employees and hire new "mind-sets" in the hope of getting better results.

Understanding this cultural field of resonance at a deeper level offers a much more powerful application for changing resonance for the human resource agenda. The corporate shadow can be transformed as it presents itself and talent can be retained and truly developed.

The use of psychological testing for new positions is H.R.'s attempt to be vigilant about unconscious and sub-conscious patterns and limitations in an applicant. At some level, they understand this relationship between personal consciousness and results.

Business is created with people of consciousness.
The consciousness of people doing business
is electrical and magnetic.

It both ATTRACTS AND REPELS results and it has
thresholds for success.

The consciousness of the people doing business
determines the limitations and non-limitations of
performance and impact.

New consciousness equals new thresholds, fewer
limitations and greater success.

Consciousness must understand its relationship
to ALL CONSCIOUSNESS AND THE
ELECTRO-MAGNETIC FIELD OF
CAUSATION to have LEVERAGE.

The concentric spheres within which we operate dictate our success in life, in business and in relationships. Simplistically, these concentric spheres are composed of our current belief systems and values, our positive and negative self-image and our old pains and pleasures.

This sphere of internal composition is magnetic and electric and attracts and repels success and failure to conform to its composition.

We create from this "our thresholds for success", our limitations and experiences that are within this sphere of experience. To move beyond these thresholds and limitations we must transform the composition of this cone or sphere of attraction.

Moving beyond this threshold of success becomes threatening and confronting and as such, sabotaging dynamics can be unconsciously introduced to keep the threshold or comfort zone in place.

Learning to become a conscious creator in our life is the new game and this means that we must become increasingly aware of our intentions, our hidden agendas, our fears and expectations and our thresholds for receiving. If we create with fear we will attract that which fear.

Everything is electromagnetic consciousness. Everything resides within a field of electromagnetic vibration. Learning about the field of our subconscious and unconscious mind becomes a critical part of the new reality game.

As we explore what it is that we are creating, the complexity of this becomes apparent. It is not an easy game to master; but master it we must.

Within our concentric spheres of creativity
we have beliefs and values,
expectations and conditionings
that we are conscious of and that are visible to us.

We also have sub-conscious and unconscious beliefs, values, expectations and conditionings that are less visible or invisible to ourselves. The goal then becomes one of becoming more conscious of what was previously hidden from us, through examining what it is that we are creating in our life.

In these times of uncertainty and as the old operating systems collapse, the world is creating its fears in frighteningly fast ways. The chaos and the overwhelm compound our personal insecurities and render us "at effect" rather than "at cause" in our life.

The only path to security is the one of new learning and new mastery. Taking the reigns of our life and learning how to create "with" the creative force of our consciousness is now the path of success.

CHAPTER EIGHT

INTEGRATION

How do you do the work of integrating your masculine and feminine consciousness? Life tries to do this for you.

Example:

- as you experience challenges or obstacles
- as you find yourself behaving in less than admirable ways
- as you obsess over "good" ways to be and suppress your authenticity
- as you feel "charged" by people or dynamics around you
- as you fail to succeed in achieving your goals
- as you repeat patterns that are stuck
- as you receive feedback
- as you recognize you are self medicating, avoiding, drinking or drugging your feelings
- as you realize your stress levels are unhealthy
- as you recognize you are unhappy

you must engage with the presenting dynamic and attend to it with thoughtfulness, deliberation and consideration.

The goal is to reach understanding. Every challenge or obstacle asks something of you. Every person who "pushes your buttons" is calling you to new understanding and new character. We can either react by being emotive and defensive or resistant or we can take our conscious awareness into each presenting challenge and respond by thinking and feeling through the issues that present and the new consciousness needed.

Seeking insight, new understanding and eventually compassion is the pathway. If you find yourself deciding an obstacle is about teaching you that the world is a place to fear and that you can't trust anyone, you are not following the right process of discovery.

Most of us, when going about our day are experiencing thoughts and feelings that create an inner dialogue and an outer conversation. When we cycle through these common patterns of dialogue and oftentimes dramas of the day, we are outside of the zone of high performance.

Further, our "backlog" of patterned information stored as our own unique self-image and model of the world with beliefs, expectations, prejudices, judgments and thresholds etc are all attached to our present day mental and emotional consciousness. This combination of electro-magnetic emotional-mind keeps us swinging between past tensions and future anxieties and for the most part out of the zone of power that is present-based and dynamically potent from integration. The swinging emotional-mind is where we must place our attention. It is calling for us to take your awareness into what we are polarized about and to find understanding, new insight and therefore new consciousness.

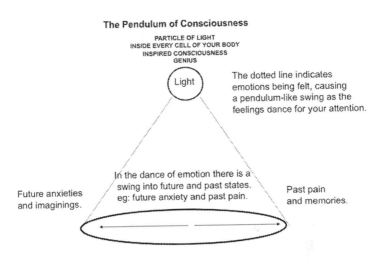

The Pendulum of Consciousness

PARTICLE OF LIGHT
INSIDE EVERY CELL OF YOUR BODY
INSPIRED CONSCIOUSNESS
GENIUS

Light

The dotted line indicates emotions being felt, causing a pendulum-like swing as the feelings dance for your attention.

In the dance of emotion there is a swing into future and past states. eg: future anxiety and past pain.

Future anxieties and imaginings.

Past pain and memories.

Insight comes from moving to a big picture view of what's happening as well as a deep in the belly understanding of the emotions that are presenting and what they are telling you. True understanding looks at each experience and within that event, examines what that event is trying to birth in you, in terms of your character.

When you have found the "true" understanding and insight into what you are "charged" about you will know because you can feel a particle/wave collapse as both polarized particles (bottom sphere) integrate and fold back into inspired consciousness (top sphere which now radiates more light.)

It can't be that "any notion will do". There is a "true understanding" waiting to be known and when you do, you enter a still-point. You will take a deep breathe, feel a release of tension a sense of knowing and then gratitude. Truth can be known and is indeed felt within.

After this integrative experience occurs there is then the ability to spend time in the Zone. How long, will depend upon how much backlog of polarized charge you contain.

As you continue to seek out your "issues, patterns and charges" and integrate them into new insight and understanding, you begin to create the "tent" of your Zone (the cone) and the more you do this, the more you can be inside your tent Zone. (Intent).

The Pendulum of Consciousness

The more you can build your Zone, the more access and availability you have to it. Less and less run by your lower consciousness charges and more in-vested in the Zone of present-tense, inspired performance.

The Law of Synchronicity
"We attract experiences to ourselves to become conscious of the limited/restricted parts of ourselves in order to transform."
Carl Jung Swiss/German psychoanalyst.

HOW DO WE GAIN INSIGHT, DISCOVERY AND UNDERSTANDING?

This is a complex subject to write about. To be understood it needs to be experienced and demonstrated. In my business trainings I use an integration process that can be taught and then self managed. In essence it begins with a questioning process. Knowing what questions to ask yourself in different situations requires practice.

What am I attracting here?

Which part of me is attracting this and why?

What beliefs or expectations am I holding that are allowing this?

What am I really "charged" about?

What is this situation "asking" of me?

What do I need to learn here?

What do I need to understand here?

What is this "birthing" in my character?

What part of me is developing itself as a result of this situation?

What is my value system?

What do I really want?

What is the truth about my feelings?

What does that say about what matters to me?

What am I supporting here?

Am I supporting something in alignment with my values?

What do I stand for?

The Dual Nature of the Masculine and Feminine

Everything that we are experiencing is an expression of the masculine and feminine. Everything that provokes us to grow is provoking us to develop something in the masculine and feminine traits.

A few examples of what may be being developed from the masculine traits are:-

Self-initiative, responsibility, accountability, personal authority, the ability to follow through, greater focus, critical thinking, contribution, new complex vision, decisiveness, financial security . . .

A few examples of what may be being developed from the feminine traits are:-

Active listening, respecting, greater conscience, team work, delegation, increased perception, deliberation, consideration, ability to share and be open, transparency, empathy, compassion, trustworthy-ness, intimacy.

We are on a journey of developing character and paradoxically transcending character; of gaining complexity and paradoxically of simplicity; of going deeper and becoming lighter.

Once a person understands the lens of examination, they can learn to do it for themselves. Some people however need assistance from others to see beyond their blind spots and gaps. This is where the Human Resource and Organizational Development function needs to step up and be run by highly aware people who can assist the growth and development of their people in effective and congruent ways.

Emotions promote the evolution of consciousness. Further, they are how we mature and grow skilled in both the EQ *and* the IQ areas of development.

Feelings and emotions are information that is essential to our development of self-knowledge. When understood they will reveal what matters to us, how to take care of ourselves and how to live our personal greatness. It is all about doing the right alchemy.

The Philosophers Stone . . . .

Turning the lead of lesser consciousness
into the gold of higher consciousness,
is the alchemical process of transforming our emotions
and our heart, our thinking and our intellect,
through a particle/wave collapse
in the cells of our body.

At energetic resonance level, there is change; at chemical levels there is change, at DNA level there is change at IQ and EQ there is change.

Understanding Feelings and Emotions

Collectively there is an aversion to feeling our emotions. Avoidances are achieved through various means . . . . restricting our breathing; using self-medication; forming habits and addictions; using prescriptions to numb; creating illness and death.

It is the incomplete feeling of those feelings; it is the incomplete thinking about those feelings; it is the incomplete understanding of those feelings that sends us down a labyrinth of tangled outcomes and tragedies.

Why are we so frightened of feeling? Collectively we will do anything we can to avoid feeling our emotions. We numb them with drugs, drink and other addictive behavior, we try and meditate them away, we try and suppress and deny them at all costs; and it is at all costs. When we refuse to engage then transform our feelings we get lost.

Our feelings give us information about our deepest selves. From our feelings we find out what matters to us, and what is important.

We find out where we are wounded and in pain. We move to defend protect ourselves with emotions such as anger and fear. We can know when our boundaries are being crossed or when damage is being done. We can discover what brings us joy or engages us with our passion. We can realize whom we care about and whom we love. Our feelings are important, essential informers from our soul.

When you refuse to give voice to your feelings, when you refuse to listen to them, you miss the clues to knowing yourself better. The journey of becoming more is one of gaining depth and substance and one of becoming more loving and at one with. Compassion and understanding can be felt and although this appears that we walk around all peaceful and radiant, that is not the case. As you become more understanding, as you integrate what is outside of you, inside of you, there is greater peace and there is a grace and wisdom, yet there is still the capacity to feel the pain of others and of the group or "collective".

The state of being at peace and in grace needs to be re-created often as the turbulent swings of the collective emotional field that we all exist within, is felt.

Each time we choose to examine our charges and integrate our issues to new understanding we are developing our masculine and feminine consciousness.

As an example of integration from discovery and insight, the woman in the earlier story who was known as a kind, generous and gentle soul, as a result of her experience with her place of work and the CEO, has become far more discerning in her relating with others and no longer sees through such rose-tinted glasses. The shadow within that organization was chauvinistic and it de-valued and deceived her. Up until that time, she had never been aware of such dynamics around her. This was her blind spot. Her need to be seen as a nice person and to not be a trouble-maker was an act of self betrayal as she allowed herself to be mistreated many times before recognizing that indeed she was being made victim to a veiled chauvinistic culture.

Newly forged instincts with greater discernment, she now sees that the experience has birthed qualities in her that are both masculine and feminine in nature. She values herself more and she questions and examines more closely the environment she finds herself in. For her, no position is worth such an act of self-betrayal again and she gives voice to her truth and her concerns early, no matter the consequences.

She protects herself better with boundaries and protocols and her ability to self promote and make visible her talents and gifts has been increased. She still has the gentle kindness of her nature but she now has the firm and assertive character traits that were in her own personal shadow self. She has evolved her consciousness; she has grown.

The corporate sector is like a Shakespearean theatre. You come up against many and varied characters and pressurized dramas that play out, "charging" you emotionally and challenging you to respond. Every emotional charge that you experience is your opportunity to integrate and grow.

Have you noticed that the things that get you all worked up don't necessarily upset others and vice versa? This is because that which "charges" you are an indication of where you lack understanding or awareness or where there are past hurts or conditionings and where you need to evolve.

Even if you pretend to not be charged, upset, or avoid that person or situation, that obstacle to your growth will show up somewhere else until you work with it. It is the nature of consciousness.

Life is set up this way to attract vibrationally what is currently calibrated, consciously, sub-consciously or unconsciously in your consciousness. This is to provoke a confrontation with yourself and promote evolution and growth through self-understanding.

When you are "charged' emotionally by an experience, you are showing yourself where your consciousness currently positions itself.

Light particles become polarized and "charged" when there is discord within the mental and emotional state. The experience of good and bad, right and wrong, pain and pleasure by its very nature is a dual or polarized event.

When we can move to insight and understanding about what we are seeing in a polarized way and we do so with true discovery, the dualized particles "fall into" each other, unifying. In physics this is called a "particle/wave collapse" or an "implosion".

When a particle/wave collapse occurs the trapped drama of consciousness (no longer charged) unites into an "aha" moment and new consciousness (understanding) is born. The light that was trapped has now not only been released but it is evolved and radiates more light. This is the everyday practical process of enlightenment. This is "illumination".

When we avoid such self-scrutiny, when we dodge and hide from what is showing up in our life whether it is in the business world or our personal lives, we stop growing. We can in fact compound lesser consciousness and the lesser behaviors and rigidly devolve in consciousness to a less integrated state. This is when manipulation, and choices made from extreme swing play out.

A leader who values transformation and does move along the path of true self-development, is a person to admire.

Many women leaders are in denial of their lack of transformation, viewing the climb to the top as proof of their growth. Yet they have actually learned how to play the game the masculine way at the detriment of their own growth. The shutdown of their genius has become so successful that their blind spot is more like a total blindness. Unfortunately, these women usually do not begin to see their imbalance until some crisis ensues and then they may begin to question and examine their hearts.

With both men and women as leaders, it is the feminine consciousness that must lead the way and the masculine powering the feminine. It is like that old saying that the feminine navigates by the stars and the masculine captains the ship. What we currently see is the masculine leading the way, the masculine powering the ship and the shadow putting gremlins in the engine.

When you invest in your own evolution; when you commit to self-development and to the path of becoming more whole, you are doing the hero's journey of life that

Joseph Campbell spoke of. This is like putting down the small story of your life and picking up the bigger one.

Here you can experience personal greatness, purposeful meaning and presence. You are conscious each day and aware of your experiences, your feelings and your feedback. You honor your feelings and use them as a compass for understanding yourself and your world.

CHAPTER NINE

THE ZONE

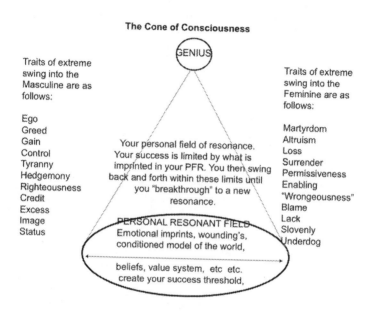

The Cone of Consciousness

GENIUS

Traits of extreme
swing into the
Masculine are as
follows:

Ego
Greed
Gain
Control
Tyranny
Hedgemony
Righteousness
Credit
Excess
Image
Status

Your personal field of resonance.
Your success is limited by what is
imprinted in your PFR. You then swing
back and forth within these limits until
you "breakthrough" to a new
resonance.

PERSONAL RESONANT FIELD.
Emotional imprints, wounding's,
conditioned model of the world,

beliefs, value system, etc etc.
create your success threshold,

Traits of extreme
swing into the
Feminine are as
follows:

Martyrdom
Altruism
Loss
Surrender
Permissiveness
Enabling
"Wrongeousness"
Blame
Lack
Slovenly
Underdog

The above diagram illustrates your field of attraction
(in the sphere at the base of the cone) and your genius
consciousness (as the smaller sphere at the top of the cone).
Either side is the extreme character traits of the Masculine
and Feminine when there is imbalanced swing.

HIGH PERFORMANCE

CONE OF CONSCIOUSNESS

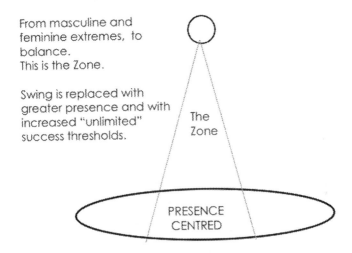

From masculine and feminine extremes, to balance.
This is the Zone.

Swing is replaced with greater presence and with increased "unlimited" success thresholds.

The Zone

PRESENCE CENTRED

As a person begins to re-evaluate their model of the world, their beliefs and expectations, their values and self-identity, the conditioned limitations of their attractive field are cleared. Not trapped by old mental and emotional dynamics, consciousness is free to reside in the centered presence of its genius.

Illuminated by the higher intelligence within, the personality then learns to navigate directions, choices and decisions from this enlightened zone.

Further, as this genius is in essence like a high voltage frequency, the person is infused with the source of power and is re-energized. A radiance, a passionate exuberance, a glowing youthfulness and a healthful cellular environment is promoted.

HIGH PERFORMANCE

CONE OF CONSCIOUSNESS

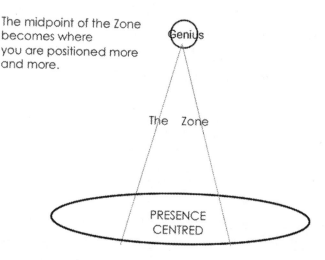

The midpoint of the Zone becomes where you are positioned more and more.

Genius

The Zone

PRESENCE CENTRED

Here you are operating in the "present tense" not in the past or in the future. The task becomes one of transforming presenting challenges into new consciousness, returning to centre and focusing on intention, expectation and productivity.

HIGH PERFORMANCE

CONE OF CONSCIOUSNESS

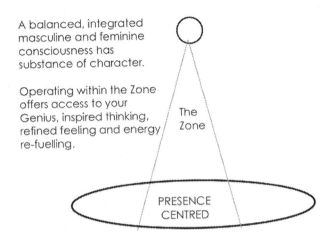

A balanced, integrated masculine and feminine consciousness has substance of character.

Operating within the Zone offers access to your Genius, inspired thinking, refined feeling and energy re-fuelling.

The Zone

PRESENCE CENTRED

A high level operator in the Zone is one who is able to create their own reality deliberately and successfully, manifesting at levels of mastery never before achieved. The person has an increased ability to pull from the higher mind's information banks and inspiration levels (finer frequency mind/consciousness) and experience, revealing wisdom, vision and a stronger congruency and alignment with the person's deeper self.

A mind that is congruent and aligned has laser-like focus and clearer manifestation skills. The person's capacity to take responsibility and achieve results is promoted and the ability to self-manage is increased.

Results that were previously unattainable are now achievable, and greater success both professionally and personally is experienced.

CHAPTER TEN

The High Performance Person /Culture

THE ORGANIZATION

Every organization desires a culture and talent base that has greater balance and maturity; one that is engaged, committed and accountable. Every organization desires a talent base with agility and resourcefulness more in evidence and the innovative, creative zone accessible, for this is a high performing culture.

The culture of your organization is the dynamic combination of the collective mind of the business entity. To change the results within your business entity you must change the collective mind . . . you must change the resonance of the collective emotional /mind.

Resonance is AT CAUSE in your business world. To change your results in business you must CHANGE THE RESONANCE of the collective cultural mind field. Consciousness and culture are companions.

How do you change the culture of your organization?

The most powerful and impactful way to effectively change the resonance of an organizational entity is to begin at the pinnacle of the organization with the CEO, the board and the senior executive. (or the person(s) who holds the business vision.)

By shifting resonance at the top of the corporate cone (concentric sphere) we get the maximum processional impact throughout the whole collective mind-field of the organization.

Like a stone thrown into a pond, its impact ripples out across the body of the water to wider and wider circles of influence . . . . when you change the mind frequency at the "top" or in the center of the organization, that change ripples out through the collective mind and impacts the whole. The higher up the corporate cone we change the resonance, the greater the impact on the whole.

Once achieved, the educational model and the tools of integration are introduced and trained into the tiered business units throughout the remaining tiers of the organizational structure. With effective targeting of the appropriate focuses for integration, resonance is elevated and the limitations of the previous cultural mindset are broken, allowing for a new success threshold.

My experience with this process over 15 years now is that when an individual is exposed to this model and experiences the freedom and power of the integration tools, there is an inherent internal commitment that emerges.

What is also appealing here is the understanding that any business group will have the greatest shift in resonance if it transforms the most disordered and emotionally charged unit within the group.

Using my Corporate Shadow module, once I have transformed the Chief Executive group I deliberately ask to work with the people who are demonstrating the most undermining or destructive behaviors within the organization. Refer back to the cone of consciousness diagram (earlier) which describes an attractive spherical field with emotional charge, mind-sets, beliefs and thresholds for success.

The laws of the new sciences here reveals that the wider the "charged" swing, the "higher the quantum leap" in consciousness if successfully transformed. Ponder the implications of this. Organizations in the greatest amount of chaos may have the most potential for growth.

Working with key performers and CEO's who have hit a crisis of sorts I can see a visible relief when I inform them that "hitting a big wall" is indicative of a big breakthrough opportunity to a new level of performance and competency. Investing the time and effort in becoming accountable for your plateaus and results leads to such great rewards that individuals and teams now eagerly seek to utilize this method whenever able in order to free-up blocks and reach for higher and higher success.

Culture change within an organization begins at the top, then moves to where there is the most discord and chaos. Then there is a tiered or unit by unit, team-by-team training process that attends to transforming the current level of consciousness.

Information, education and integration at a significant level, must then occur in all global offices, following the same blueprint.

The densest levels of mind become less dense, shifting to higher octaves of resonance and attracting better results. The finer frequency minds shift to a higher octave of resonance, attracting higher levels of success. The more minds with higher octave frequencies of resonance, the greater the inspiration, innovation and productivity levels within the organization.

Each new cultural concentric sphere operates with a new set of attractions and repulsions thus a new level of performance is achieved . . . . results that were previously unattainable are now achievable, and greater success both professionally and personally is experienced.

(This is assuming the transformation has been to *greater* complexity balance, and inspiration. Some cultures transform to lesser complexity more imbalance and stress.)

The corporate shadow is transformed and what was subconscious becomes conscious with the experience of deeper insights, intuition and clarity. The ability to focus, direct energy and take action is increased and a higher level of productivity can then be realized.

YOUR BUSINESS
IS INSIDE AN ELECTROMAGNETIC FIELD.
IT'S RESONANCE **CAUSES**
YOUR BUSINESS SUCCESS AND FAILURE.

New consciousness equals new productivity. The leader who invests in the consciousness of its people is the leader who invests in the longevity and profitability of the business. Transforming the spheres of productivity in the organization provides sustained profits and success.

HUMAN RESOURCES & ORGANIZATIONAL DEVELOPMENT

The HR and OD areas within organizations must be trained to support and maintain the new model of a high performance culture. Commonly this group within a business entity is lacking and needing new learning's and understandings.

As this group is usually the deciding body that implements training and development there must be a solid foundation of knowledge and a consistent approach to building a successful culture. Too often the platform within HR and OD shifts and changes as the "new trend" appears.

This model is not a "new trend". It is a revolutionary paradigm shift that rewrites the psychology of performance and the nature of reality; an important and fundamental difference.

The integration process that I use in executive trainings has applications across all areas including:

- Linking the vision of the individual with the company vision
- Conflict resolution
- Clearing resentments/disputes with the business entity
- Leadership issues/clarity/strength

- Establishing order during peak "change" periods
- Nourishing company culture, providing stability and long-term benefits
- Clearing issues that are "charged"
- Keeping a "big picture" perspective within the organization with respect to economic fluctuations and global swings
- Offers a human resource application that accelerates the growth, effectiveness and consciousness of the organization

To stay consistent and support the high performance culture, human resources must be committed to the new model and equipped with the integration process (IP) that applies across all applications.

Personal responsibility for performance and self-empowerment must be fostered so that each individual is accountable for his or her own journey within the corporate entity. Conflict resolution must be facilitated via the IP model.

Seeding this new approach to business operations and productivity is essential for the long-term success of such a transformation. Alignment and congruency across all lines of service will encourage the coherence necessary for sustainability.

Developing an emotional ecology of this nature within an organization means that the new concepts will need to be "seeded, fertilized and weeded" consistently to establish a good root system. Overcoming the long-held avoidance of confrontation and self-examination is necessary and a willingness to build relationships of curiosity, learning, transparency and trust.

There is a charted execution plan. It is about transforming our business cultures tier by tier from their previously emotional adolescence into adulthood and maturity and implementing the integration process into all systems.

Those who have "senior" roles within the corporate entity must be aware of their particular role within the organization. Those who hold positions of leadership have achieved these roles because they are at a level of consciousness that is ready to integrate behavior at greater levels of complexity. Their mindset should be operating at a higher level of complex integration and productivity. They should be able to direct conflict and charge through examining performance issues and assist their direct reports to new consciousness.

HR can utilize this model from the start of an interview process, to the managing of conflict and performance and then on to the exit strategy. Organizational culture attracts towards it, employees with resonant emotional/mind-sets that match those within the combined concentric sphere of the business entity.

When applicants seek out positions through the interview process they are unconsciously drawn to those business groups that reflect the same resonance as them and are not attracted to those that do not. We all feel this when we come out of an interview and have had an immediate sense of "rightness" or "wrongness" about the meeting and how the cultural environment feels.

If our resonance does not fall between the base level consciousness and the highest-level consciousness of the organization we will not be successful in being hired. There is an unconscious collusion in the interviewer and the interviewee to find that fit. Therefore, whichever business environment you find yourself in it will reflect back to you components of what you hold within your own subconscious and unconscious mind.

INTEGRATING TEAMS

Now lets look at another story I often tell, where I am called to work with the sales team of a multi-national. This particular team had a major grievance with their newly appointed National Sales Manager. He was sharp, abrupt, bordering on bullying and barked orders that he simply expected to be followed.

Previous to this manager the group had the same National Sales Manager for 5 years and they had bonded strongly. This fellow was someone who had well developed feminine competencies. His ability to actively listen, get to know his people, understand their talents and needs and motivate accordingly was praised. His team had a sense of belonging and they were treated with great respect so there was loyalty, trust and that elusive discretionary X factor. Everyone wanted to do well for him and the numbers illustrated his success. Many in the sales team accessed naturally the Zone that I spoke of and they were a highly profitable group.

Now with a new National Sales Manager I was called in to do some conflict resolution work and I asked them into a full day of development. I took them through the integration process where each person wrote a list of all of the grievances they had with the new NSM. It was a private written process. Then I had each of them examine what every grievance was challenging in them in terms of learning and development.

Throughout this stage of the process the energy in the room began to shift. One by one they discovered unique to themselves how this manager was benefiting them. I had taken them through the dual competencies of the masculine and feminine psyche and overall the realization was that the new manager was developing competencies in the masculine domain.

Some were learning to confront and voice their truth, others were learning to go into greater detail and analysis, others more responsibility and accountability.

They were stunned by the results. I explained to them that there are always plateaus in growth and performance and when we plateau we attract in a challenge that pushes us beyond the stuck points to a new level of operation. This team had gone a long way in developing their feminine competencies and although they had good masculine skills the next growth curve was about taking those skills to greater acuity and meticulousness.

Each person in that room felt the truth of the new awareness. They realized that they were not the victims of a new manager to suffer through but that this was a natural pattern of attraction. They realized that there was some other force at play in life that was a guiding principle that they could trust.

Ponder this for a moment. This is an extraordinary outcome.

Next I worked one on one with the NSM and of course, his grievances about his new team were all challenging him to develop competencies in the feminine domain.

Active listening, empathy, creating relationship, engaging with respect and learning receptivity were all part of his "feminine" learning curve. He too felt congruence about this within himself.

Needless to say, the entire dynamics of this situation changed. The team and the NSM approached each other with a new maturity and gravity. Within a short time they were "firing on all cylinders" and they were able to access more and more of the zone of inspired success.

SALES

Sales teams are often those that can lead the way in this high performance paradigm. The sales people that "live or die" by the results on the board have had to master their mind-set and work with affirming inner dialogue to lift their magnetism to attract the sale. Consciously or unconsciously they have been exploring this model of attraction and of the Zone. Where most of their efforts to-date, relied on manipulating their state, now they can be shown a way to "be" the state authentically, because of the internal shifting that takes place. Instinctively sales teams love this model and take the lead.

As the marketplace strains with the ramifications of economic calamity, the challenge for those in the business of selling is great. Giving power away to the outside world moves the seller into a "victim of" and into the old Newtonian world where things are "done to them". This paradigm is outdated and based on inadequate information. To hold to this stance is to slip away into a world of greater struggle and loss. Fear becomes a potent game player and the more tragedy and chaos is witnessed the more the "victim" is being "done to" and power remains outside.

Equipping sales teams with the breakthrough discoveries of this model enables them to operate with greater effortless success.

MERGERS

The integration process is very successful with cross culture cohesion. With the increase in mergers occurring between companies today and the need to have a coherent culture operating within a short time-span such a tool facilitates the integration of both cultures into a third culture that is resourceful agile and diverse.

Whenever mergers occur, the developmental theme for all who are involved in the experience is to develop themselves through interaction with the new behaviors and values. Consciously participating in this as early as possible fast tracks the learning's and "anchors in" the resulting competencies.

When two cultures meet, the earlier diagram becomes as two cones with the lower concentric spheres of operation overlapping to create a third concentric sphere. As integration occurs the overlap gets wider and wider until fusion has occurred.

We are in revolutionary times . . . .
our world has changed and so
too has our business landscape.
In this climate of heightened instability,
the chaos and turbulence of these times
insist that we learn quickly what the new rules are
to secure and sustain success.

THE INDIVIDUAL HIGH PERFORMER

The corporate/business arena is another theatre where your "charges" can be triggered to provoke your attention. In playing out the limitations or dramas in this theatre, your consciousness seeks an opportunity to evolve. The business arena is another feedback mechanism for letting you know where you are limited in your personal mindset and presenting you with opportunities to go beyond your current reality creations and attract more inspired, fulfilling realities.

It is a theatre for self-exploration that offers you countless opportunities to enlighten your mind and expand your being. An enlightened mind leads to an open hearted, inspired life, creatively and dynamically.

Your "success" or "failure" in your business arena is decided by the resonance of your mindset . . . . your internal picture of reality.

What feedback are you getting in you work about?

- your effectiveness?
- your service or product?
- your market place?
- your business colleagues?
- your team's effectiveness?

INDIVIDUAL CRISIS

Perhaps you have been impacted by the economic collapse to such a degree that you are out of work and experiencing crisis. This asks of you that you do a "descent" into the imprints in your attractive field. You will need to follow a very important process of transformation.

Write down in a column, all that you believe about yourself and your self-image. Be thorough and write down all of the "darkest" thoughts and feelings about yourself and your results and experiences to date. Unfortunately this is best done with some assistance to reach the deeper truths and discoveries but this is the best we can do in a book. Once you have listed this, add to that list your current reality issues and experiences.

Next, take some time to examine each one on the list and discover using the questions in the earlier chapter of the book, what you are needing to understand or re evaluate or shift in your thinking and feeling.

Ultimately I believe that the world is experiencing a changing of the guard. The feminine power is taking its rightful place as the lead navigator. For many people who are in crisis and loss, there will be a profound motivation towards creating their life anew with the right partnership. Surrendering the feeling of separation and victim, of powerlessness and desperation and opening to feeling the union with a power source within, these people can make strides in re-creating their lives in ways never before witnessed.

Dig deep, examine and confront all wounds, all emotional pain and trauma and find the treasure of what these experiences are birthing in you. Then look at where they are leading you. You will begin to change your beliefs and expectations and you will feel lifted, on purpose and with meaning.

List all of your talents, gifts and passions. Formulate intention that aligns with what you have discovered in your writing process. In a humble state of Grace, ask your inner intelligence to guide you. Slow down, centre and allow for the mystery of what emerges. If you cannot move to joy, work with gratitude. Gratitude will move you away from fear to a resonance where you can access the Zone of your genius. Let your life and your success be created through you. Integrating charge to new understanding is an ongoing process.

Your personal and collective issues, limiting
paradigms, expectations
and desires are all reflected back to you in your results
in your business and your entire life.
Your "success" or "failure" in your business arena is
feedback
to you about the mindset that you are operating within.
Master your world by understanding the big picture.
All the world is a stage!

All are feedback experiences that indicate where opportunities are being presented to this person to move to a higher concentric sphere of operation. This produces higher consciousness that then shifts their resonance to a higher success level ratio. They breakthrough to new levels of success.

If an individual is not growing and developing they leave themselves open to being challenged by any direct report or outside talent who may hold a complexity of emotional mind that is greater than theirs.

The person with the higher resonance will either be promoted in time, or another outside person will be hired to take their place. If a direct report is developing "past" their reporting person and not being managed to develop further this can cause problems. More commonplace is key talent that is innovative and inspired with a well-balanced masculine and feminine nature. The manager fails to recognize that their driver is feminine and as such their productivity is thwarted or shut down.

I have consulted to groups where talent chooses to "coach upwards" in an attempt to develop understanding in those in senior roles. Not wanting to move beyond the role they find satisfying but frustrated by feeling "hamstrung" in their productivity they struggle with reporting lines that are inadequate in understanding how to support their modus operandi.

Often such people do not believe that they can find a different business culture with a better resonance that will support them so they remain. Defeated in their belief that all business cultures are essentially the same. Over time their stress levels increase, work satisfaction decreases and not only can they not find that highly productive Zone but their energy is being drained from grievance and frustration.

What we have is a depleted and diminished productivity and a wasted loss of focus and invention. With all of our revolutionary understandings of human performance and of the nature of reality there is no excuse now for not cultivating a new business paradigm and a new world dream.

CHAPTER ELEVEN

THE INDIVIDUAL AND THE ZONE

Leadership can be exhibited by every individual regardless of title or position. With a spirit of conscious attention to personal impact, effort and engagement the individual can cultivate a leadership dynamic within themselves.

Understanding that the Zone of high performance is the elite state of being that maximizes and leverages "success" offers the individual a valuable map for reaching for personal greatness.

To access the Zone a person needs to feel enthusiasm and dynamic energy for their life in as many arenas as possible. We have all heard repeatedly that it is important to "do what you love". This is because loving what you are doing automatically steps you into the Zone of high performance.

Each of us has an inherent Creative Force that IS OUR FUNCTIONING. We function BEST when we are generating and following the nature of that force ("may the force be with you.")

Children are best assisted when they have parents and teachers that are able to observe their strengths, their unique nature and inclinations and their joys and passions. All of the keys and clues to their Creative functioning are visible in the early years. The task is to find those keys and clues and to encourage, promote and expand upon those inherent indicators.

Judgment and bias need to step aside for the freedom and opening up of a child's best functioning. If we impose our own agendas upon children believing that we know what is best for them, their core functioning can become submerged and lost. Parents too often inflict a reductive rationale on their children via processes such as analyzing the market place for the safe and profitable career direction and imposing generational restrictions that follow the family traditions.

A child must then suppress their self-generating Creative force and go against their own natural drives and expression. This causes an energetic shut down that begins to move the child further and further away from their right and true path of functioning. Unhappiness, stress, dis-ease and depression can result. Anger and defiance can be a valid unconscious retaliation from children who know that something is wrong. Others may turn that anger in on themselves with a resulting loss of esteem and confidence.

Going against the right course requires a huge amount of effort. Energy flows and generates freely when it is being expressed and is allowed its functioning in ever-more creative and productive ways. Not allowing this functioning it's expression, shuts the energy and life force down to a trickle. To then impose an unwanted and wrongly directed function on that person who is operating on just a "trickle" of their natural energy source creates stressful dynamics.

Consider the effort it takes to study a subject you have no interest in. Consider the energy it takes to focus and concentrate on a task or learning that you have no natural inclination for or is even outside your ability to excel in.

Our patriarchal, masculine value system insists that the signs of success and of a valuable human being are found in status and image. Safe, controllable, ordered, secure career decisions offering options, substantial monetary reward and a hierarchical job trajectory are the valued, reasonable and rational career paths.

This patriarchal value system has infiltrated our advertising, our school systems, our business cultures and our relationships. The argument for distorting and morphing our children into forms that are better suited to succeed in another contorted system continues. Yet it is rooted in ignorant and flawed assumptions that promote an unhealthy and destructive society.

Prescription drugging of our children is at epidemic proportions. Violence, crime, teenage depression, self-abuse and homelessness is on the rise. Adults as mentioned in the earlier chapter are self-medicating, taking pharmaceutical drugs, on short and long term dis-ability leave, waking day to day in varying degrees of unhappiness as they go to a job they dislike and cant wait for the day to be over.

If we made it a priority to be in our natural state of thriving, and demanded this of ourselves and our work, the picture would be very different.

Imagine a world where there is a core understanding of how we as human beings function, creatively, productively and inspirationally. Where our psychology and performance books are all written in support of this understanding. Where our educational systems, our teachers with the parents and children are all tasked with seeking the natural, inherent talents and joys of each other and in promoting their expression and cultivation. Were society's value system a balanced merging of the masculine and feminine the world would be a different place. Being and living in the zone of dynamic energy where passion is accessed, complex genius is available and innovative vision is found, would be inspired living in the fullest.

People would rise in the morning, eager to engage in their day and fueled by the enthusiasm and purposefulness of being aligned with their true functioning. There would be a meaning and a fulfillment inherent in the experience of living and working.

"Appreciative Inquiry" is a model that is fast becoming accepted and utilized in the business world. This model has at its core a focus on promoting the strengths and unique talents within an individual and on that which promotes that individuals health, vitality and success. This is a good step in the right direction.

360 review, performance and psychological testing has for so long been used to highlight "weaknesses" in a person that must then be zeroed in on for strengthening and development. Whilst some measure of this can be valid and useful for a person the measure of this must be if the person themselves has a willing energetic desire to incorporate this strengthening into themselves; and indeed if this strengthening will add to a persons inspired state.

Too often a person is asked to become competent in a full 360 spectrum of skills both hard and soft. When this requires the individual to move so far away from their natural functioning that the result is energy shut down and long term stress, the persons core strengths become impacted. An individual may be very competent at accounting and math and naturally prone to being introverted and reflective. Insisting that this person develop public speaking skills to participate in networking and marketing for their firm could cause the person to move into so much fear and self doubt that their focus on their accounting practice is reduced.

For some, this request may be received with some trepidation but overall a real eagerness to develop and grow in this area of competency. For them, they are ready and willing to expand in this way and it will therefore add to their Creative dynamic in a positive way.

For others they may need more time or indeed may never want to grow in that direction. For them, perhaps listening to that call to stay functioning in a more insular and reflective way is one that keeps them feeling safe and okay. They have no desire to follow a ladder of achievement or add more work challenges to their goals. Their path of function is slower and more introverted than others and should be valued just as much. For every person who thrives on challenge, change and innovation there is a person who keeps to a steadfast, reliable, risk-averse format. Both are needed, both are valuable, both are balance.

Alternatively, another person may choose to be happy with certain confines of a role because their true work is not "at work" but "outside" of work. Their family may be where their natural functioning and growth is happening, or with their loving relationship. Perhaps they are involved in a church, a hobby, another interest or group that is where their inspiration is ignited. Note that I am truly speaking to being inspired and joyous or where there is natural inclination, talent and gift that can be a path to joy and inspiration. I am not speaking of duty, obligation or service that is from any foundation of "should" or conditioned attendance.

We need to begin promoting new values with a new measurement system that rewires our brains and our minds to have permission to seek out the freeing and liberating choices that lead to real joy, authenticity and inspiration.

The Steps to Living and Working in a Zone Inspired Life

Step 1
Love who you are.

This is key. If you find you are constantly doubting and berating yourself, lacking self-esteem and self-worth you MUST heal this.

Start with drawing up a list of all the negative character traits that you believe you have and of all of the negative events and experiences that you have had. Include any character traits that you think you SHOULD have and feel you are not demonstrating.

Take that list and quietly and thoughtfully work through it. One at a time, read the negative you have written and ask yourself how that "negative" actually SERVES you. What does it offer you?

Everything serves us in some way. Even if it is simply as the only tool we have at that time to cope, its serves us until we learn a better way.

For each "negative" event, ask yourself what this is "birthing" in your character . . . . in a positive sense.

Events can "birth" in us so many things. Self awareness, self protection, self care, a need to value ourselves more, a voice to protest or to stand up for ourselves. Experiences can call us to be more honoring, to be more responsible, to make new choices. A situation can foster a desire to learn and seek knowledge, to move in another direction or to perhaps that we need to seek out support and ask for help.

As you move through your list, your task is to create a process of discovery; be curious and be thorough. If you are reaching points of insight and clarity you will also be revealing to yourself some highlighted truths about your personal path and who you are becoming. A simple example of this is the young boy who lived an early childhood of mis-treatment and tragedy. As a young teenager one particular event characterized by injustice and betrayal seemed to tip the scales of his life. All of the past pains and treatment came together to propel him into the study of law. He became a Supreme Court Judge later in life with a reputation for being just and principled.

Another example that is more subtle is of a young girl whose early life was characterized by critical and harsh parents leading to a pattern of self sabotaging success and relationships. Her life was calling her to foster self-love. She needed to learn how to be kind to her self, to be compassionate about her limits and vulnerabilities and to choose friends and relations that were good to her. Her work needed to be rewarding and allow her to grow in self-esteem.

We all come in many shapes, sizes and with different, strengths, sensitivities and functioning. Work through the list until you can feel self-acceptance through insight and discovery. Then each day make choices that foster self-love.

Step 2
Love what you do.

Seek out your Creative energy and discover its nature and function. If you have found this, you will know by the joy you feel when you are doing it. Find a recipe for doing what you love that allows you to thrive and take care of yourself and your life. The recipe and the formula will change at various stages of your life. Your task is to have the formula of your life weighted in the joyous and inspired feelings so that you are living and working in the Zone.

If you are finding this difficult to fathom or accomplish, use the Zone as your tool for finding your formula. If you can be in a joyous or loving state, sit in stillness and quiet your mind from the chatter of the day. If possible drop into alpha state, that dreamier state you can often feel when on long drives in a car. Ask your inner intelligence to show you the way to a thriving and abundant formula. Do this daily for a number of days and watch and listen for direction. The direction will be quiet and heart opening when it comes. (It is not a sudden "wow, I think I will leave my family, stow away on a ship and live on a deserted island!" This is a fantasy ego-based voice not your higher intelligence.)

Step 3
Fuel and generate your Creative Zone daily.

Give it your focus, your attention and your craft. Share your energy, create and produce with it freely. Give your Creative energy what it needs in terms of the right food, water, nutrients, exercise and love.

On rising, consciously focus on what you are grateful for and on what you love. As you move through your morning, note what you need to lift to enthusiasm and joy. Give yourself what you need. Quiet time to gather yourself, connection time to engage with others, dressing a particular way to feel authentic and good, setting the environment around you with scents, news, fresh air and sunlight, coffee and boardrooms. Get to know what you need to generate your energy, step into that Zone and sustain it.

Step 4
Manage being present.

If you find that you are out of alignment and off centre, caught up perhaps in future anxieties or past pains, stop and sort yourself back to "present tense". Draw up a list of the negatives that are bothering you and find with each one what they are offering you, teaching you, or trying to birth in you.

When you feel you have discovered the true insights to each issue you will feel calm again, centred and good. Move to feeling gratitude and take the steps you need to take to get to joy and back into the Zone.

Gratitude is the greatest tool for opening up the door to your higher Creative Zone. It doesn't matter how "down" you are there is always so much to be grateful for. Be thankful that you have working limbs, eyes that have sight, ears that can hear music and laughter. Be thankful for living in a free society or for having access to water and good air. In your deepest darkest times go to the basics and be grateful.

Step 5
Manage your electro–magnetic energy.

Become conscious of how people and environments affect your energy. Everyone is different and is impacted differently. The task is to maximize your energy and minimize exposure to environments that deplete it.

Office environments can be hazardous to electromagnetic energy. Florescent lights, open plan layouts, lack of natural light and fresh air can all impact certain people by depleting their field. This then affects concentration and stress levels, thwarting access to high performance.

There are people who cannot work inside a building all day. They need open air, or movement or physical labor to feel happy and to thrive.

Everyone we meet challenges our energy. When two energies meet there is a tousle of positioning. Both energies can meet at the lowest level, the highest level or somewhere in the middle. If you find you are constantly in the company of people that you drop in energy around, there is something to examine and pay attention to. It can be a slippery slide downhill into lesser expression and behavior and a hard climb back to your level ground.

Illness by its very nature depletes the electromagnetic field within the body. This means that our ability to attract and magnetize our reality is depleted. It must become a priority to restore health and wholeness to ensure optimum attraction.

Step 6
Build a relationship with your inner Genius

This is not your ego, but your inspired, compassionate inner wisdom. To really live in the Zone and cultivate personal greatness you must build a relationship with that greatness that resides in your genius.

We are speaking to a partnership that is hierarchical. Your Genius is YOU at a higher frequency of wisdom. This

YOU needs to be the authority and guide in your life. Your personality is you at a lower frequency of expression. It needs to be the messenger that carries out the direction of the Genius.

You can ask questions and seek clarity from your Genius by shifting your feelings and formulating a simple statement, then keep asking the question until you get the answer.

Innovative business people are naturally accessing this Zone and have a well-developed relationship with their Creative Genius though it may not be conscious. They have a way of creating the environment and the state of being that opens up access and then of holding a question or a problem in a free flowing way until clarity, solution of creativity "drops in".

Deadlines and timelines can inhibit this process and it requires a certain level of mastery to bypass this. When problem solving or seeking innovation or solution you have to step into the zone of "presence". You cannot be present and worrying about a deadline or timeline at the same time. You must "let go" of the concern or anxiety component within the dynamic and immerse yourself in the substance of the quest. It can be like "flying by the seat of your pants" because you need to let uncertainty, feelings of powerlessness or failure be part of the dynamic but not inhibit.

Classically "operators" prefer to feel in control and like the security of this feeling. It is merely an illusion however and control and creativity, or control and genius cannot co-exist in the same space and time.

Step 7
Cultivate a state of "wonder".

Wonder is an exceptional state of being. It can transcend the limited frequencies of the everyday mind-set and lift a person into a different domain of experience. Wonder opens up access to serendipity, awe and magnificence. It also fosters humility, innocence and intimacy. This domain adds a richness and a textural quality to our lives that is its own reward.

IN CONCLUSION

A change in consciousness must lead the way into our individual lives, into a new business culture and into the global leadership scene. If we are to transform the critical challenges that lie ahead for us with the intricacies of sustaining and creating growth across all territories, we must stand down the masculine captaincy with its reductive, myopic lens and place a new captain in charge. Then, together with the right roles and alliance and collaboration, we can forge the maps to inspired living and a healthy world.

This book is a call to re-examine the established paradigm in our western culture and it is a call to re-examine ourselves. The feminine wisdom and its ability for enhanced perception and complexity is an earned lens.

The earning comes with the continuing process of questioning, of on-going examination and integration. It asks you to think, feel and to face; to move beyond the common denials and justifications and to engage with a mature intent to grow and to understand. It comes with learning to function in a whole new way and with enabling your genius to emerge.

As this "sleeping giant" wakes up, and is properly integrated with the masculine consciousness within us all, a powerful partnership can develop. The masculine mind, matured with the substance and complexity of the integrated feminine heart, matures.

With a tempered wisdom and a balanced outlook, a conscience is born that oversees decisions, actions and choices. A vision emerges that inherently contains within it an understanding of the complex interconnected layers. A powerful active dynamic is demonstrated that grounds vision into reality and focuses inspiration into manifestation. A Zone is accessed that brings genius into play and expanding possibility and potential through the power of synergy.

This powerful consciousness will change the world of business and the way of the world. It releases innovation, passion, creativity and sustained productivity, free of the shackles of control and suppressive manipulations.

This powerful partnership, of both the feminine and the masculine consciousness in alliance, is the hope of our future.

Yvonne Evans
Personal–Corporate–Global
Consciousness

Website
www.yvonneevans.net

OKANAGAN REGIONAL LIBRARY
3 3132 03644 8183